**New Directions for
Community Colleges**

Arthur M. Cohen
EDITOR-IN-CHIEF

Caroline Q. Durdella
Nathan R. Durdella
ASSOCIATE EDITORS

The College Completion Agenda: Practical Approaches for Reaching the Big Goal

Brad C. Phillips
Jordan E. Horowitz

EDITORS

Number 164 • Winter 2013
Jossey-Bass
San Francisco

THE COLLEGE COMPLETION AGENDA: PRACTICAL APPROACHES FOR REACHING THE BIG GOAL
Brad C. Phillips, Jordan E. Horowitz (eds.)
New Directions for Community Colleges, no. 164

Arthur M. Cohen, Editor-in-Chief
Caroline Q. Durdella, Nathan R. Durdella, Associate Editors

NEW DIRECTIONS FOR COMMUNITY COLLEGES (ISSN 0194-3081, electronic ISSN 1536-0733) is part of The Jossey-Bass Higher and Adult Education Series and is published quarterly by Wiley Subscription Services, Inc., A Wiley Company, at Jossey-Bass, One Montgomery St., Ste. 1200, San Francisco, CA 94104. POSTMASTER: Send address changes to New Directions for Community Colleges, Jossey-Bass, One Montgomery St., Ste. 1200, San Francisco, CA 94104.

SUBSCRIPTIONS cost $89 for individuals in the U.S., Canada, and Mexico, and $113 in the rest of the world for print only; $89 in all regions for electronic only; $98 in the U.S., Canada, and Mexico for combined print and electronic; $122 for combined print and electronic in the rest of the world. Institutional print only subscriptions are $311 in the U.S., $351 in Canada and Mexico, and $385 in the rest of the world; electronic only subscriptions are $311 in all regions; combined print and electronic subscriptions are $357 in the U.S., $397 in Canada and Mexico, and $431 in the rest of the world.

EDITORIAL CORRESPONDENCE should be sent to the Editor-in-Chief, Arthur M. Cohen, at 1749 Mandeville Lane, Los Angeles, CA 90049. All manuscripts receive anonymous reviews by external referees.

New Directions for Community Colleges is indexed in CIJE: Current Index to Journals in Education (ERIC), Contents Pages in Education (T&F), Current Abstracts (EBSCO), Ed/Net (Simpson Communications), Education Index/Abstracts (H. W. Wilson), Educational Research Abstracts Online (T&F), ERIC Database (Education Resources Information Center), and Resources in Education (ERIC).

Microfilm copies of issues and articles are available in 16mm and 35mm, as well as microfiche in 105mm, through University Microfilms Inc., 300 North Zeeb Road, Ann Arbor, MI 48106-1346.

CONTENTS

EDITORS' NOTES

Study after study has shown that postsecondary education is associated with higher earnings; unfortunately, the United States fares poorly among other industrialized nations in postsecondary attainment. In 2008, among other industrialized nations, the United States ranked 12th for citizens aged 25–34; and only 29.4% of our African American population and 19.2% of our Hispanic population aged 25–34 had an associate degree or higher (College Board, 2013). In response to these concerns, the Obama administration early on set forth a goal of America having the highest proportion of college graduates in the world as part of efforts to revive the national economy. This was followed by a $20 million grant program to address the issue under the Fund for the Improvement of Postsecondary Education (FIPSE). Other federal funding initiatives followed.

With the lead of the federal government, a national College Completion Agenda developed. The Lumina Foundation weighed in and established its Big Goal to "increase the percentage of Americans with high-quality [two- or four-year college] degrees and credentials [from 39% of the population] to 60% by the year 2025" (Russell, 2011, p. 3), an increase of 23 million graduates above current rates. In response, postsecondary associations, funders, and institutions have joined forces in many ways to define the issue and identify solutions. These national completion initiatives include, among others, the following: The College Completion Agenda sponsored by the College Board; Access to Success sponsored by the National Association of System Heads and Education Trust; Complete College America sponsored by a consortium of funders including the Carnegie Corporation, Bill and Melinda Gates Foundation, Lumina Foundation, W. K. Kellogg Foundation, and Ford Foundation; and Achieving the Dream (Russell, 2011). These national initiatives have done a good job of defining the problem, raising awareness, proposing solutions, and supporting efforts to increase completion. However, the recommendations tend to be general.

In this volume of *New Directions for Community Colleges*, we present practical strategies and solutions drawn from the field to advance the College Completion Agenda. Each of these strategies and solutions addresses a key aspect of colleges that can be the focus of efforts to support the College Completion Agenda. Some address the internal world of America's colleges, such as the role of leadership or using data, while others address the context within which our colleges act—linking to high school college readiness efforts or partnering with other institutions to collaborate on defining student learning outcomes at the discipline and degree level. Some strategies are designed to improve student achievement for those at great risk for noncompletion—students in remedial or developmental courses—and

NEW DIRECTIONS FOR COMMUNITY COLLEGES, no. 164, Winter 2013 © 2014 Wiley Periodicals, Inc.
Published online in Wiley Online Library (wileyonlinelibrary.com) • DOI: 10.1002/cc.20075

other strategies are designed to improve academic completion rates for all students. Some focus on academic factors and others focus on nonacademic student supports.

What all of these have in common, though, is their intentional design to improve the likelihood that students will persist to a college degree. These are not initiatives designed primarily to raise awareness, mobilize support, or promote legislation. These are strategies and solutions implemented locally at the institutional level to improve student completion rates at colleges.

Furthermore, these strategies and solutions are designed to ensure a focus on quality. Many commentators, pundits, and critics have noted that a focus solely on the outcome of completion rates can sacrifice quality for achieving a target. The chapters in this volume demonstrate that quality is a necessary aspect of increasing completion rates. The focus is on understanding and improving the student experience so completion becomes the likely outcome of enrollment.

The foreword by Walter G. Bumphus, president and chief executive officer of the American Association of Community Colleges, describes the College Completion Agenda—its development, evolution, and progress to date. Bumphus also places the Completion Agenda in a historical context.

The first chapter, by renowned college chancellor/president Byron N. McClenney, addresses the issue of leadership. McClenney presents lessons learned about the central role college leaders fulfill in moving the completion agenda forward. One could argue that each subsequent chapter is dependent on McClenney's.

The next three chapters address internal systems and functions that chief executives of community colleges can examine at their own institutions. The first discusses the role and uses of data. Phillips and Horowitz discuss the importance of data to understanding the impact of policies and practices designed to move the completion agenda forward. The authors argue that although data collection, storage, and reporting systems must be useful and usable, creating a data-driven culture must also include understanding how individuals process information and promoting organizational habits. They draw upon their decade's worth of experience at the Institute for Evidence-Based Change working with colleges to use evidence to drive improvement.

In the next chapter, Jenkins and Cho discuss the critical importance of helping college students enter into a program of study as soon as they enter college. They argue for a continuous redesign process and extend the previous chapter's focus on collecting data in support of evidence-based improvement. Both authors are researchers at the Community College Research Center at Teachers College, Columbia University, focusing on student persistence, retention, and completion.

In the third, Venezia and Hughes discuss reforming developmental education at our nation's colleges. Also referred to as remedial or precollege courses, the authors argue that current practices work against completion. They present alternative strategies being tested at colleges around the country demonstrating early success in moving students to college-level coursework and, ultimately, completion. Both authors have been researching the issue, including the student perspective on advancing through remedial education, for many years. Venezia is an associate professor of Public Policy and Administration at the California State University, Sacramento, and the associate director of the University's Institute for Higher Education Leadership & Policy. Hughes is the executive director of Community College and Higher Education Initiatives at the College Board.

The next two chapters encourage college leadership to work with partners external to their institutions. Valdez and Marshall discuss the need for colleges to partner with feeder high school districts to align high school exit expectations with college entrance expectations. They make the case that the Common Core State Standards can support these efforts, but unless discussions occur between the two segments, alignment is left too much to chance. They illustrate the impact of alignment with a partnership that resulted in the English Curriculum Alignment Project (ECAP), which led to reduced placement into remediation and greater academic success in college English courses. Valdez and Marshall work closely with intersegmental professional learning councils throughout the nation.

Kolb, Kalina, and Chapman present Tuning—an effort that brings colleges and four-year institutions together to define student learning outcomes (SLOs) within disciplines for associate, bachelor, and master degree levels. Funded primarily by the Lumina Foundation, the outputs of Tuning are designed to improve college completion by aligning assessments, curricula, and courses to agreed-upon SLOs and clarifying expectations for students. The effort also eases transfers among institutions (including from two- to four-year institutions) because there are agreed-upon degree expectations. Kolb is a project officer for Tuning USA at the Lumina Foundation, Kalina was the vice president for Tuning USA at the Institute for Evidence-Based Change, and Chapman was a Tuning associate.

The volume closes with a discussion of financial aid by Julia I. Lopez. Lopez is the president and CEO of the College Access Foundation of California, which is a large private foundation committed to increasing the number of low-income students who attend and complete college across the state. In the chapter, she discusses the importance of financial aid to supporting the completion agenda and includes the personal perspective from students.

Brad C. Phillips
Jordan E. Horowitz
Editors

References

College Board. (2013). *The college completion agenda: Gaining leadership in postsecondary degree attainment.* New York, NY: Author.

Russell, A. (2011). *A guide to major U.S. college completion initiatives.* Washington, DC: American Association of Colleges and Universities.

BRAD C. PHILLIPS *is the president and CEO of the Institute for Evidence-Based Change and a data coach for Achieving the Dream.*

JORDAN E. HOROWITZ *is the vice president for Foundation Relations and Project Development with the Institute for Evidence-Based Change and formerly senior project director in Evaluation Research at WestEd.*

Foreword

Walter G. Bumphus

American higher education now faces greater challenges than at any time in its history. But those challenges are balanced by unprecedented opportunity to reinvent the way we collectively serve students. More research has been done . . . more philanthropic dollars have been invested . . . more innovative technologies have been applied. These factors, complemented by growing receptiveness among educators to provide greater transparency predicated on a culture of evidence, are transforming the academy.

Nowhere is this more evident than in the nation's community colleges. For most of their more than 112-year history, two-year institutions received little attention in terms of research or analysis relating to institutional effectiveness on their campuses. Instead the focus was mainly on affordability, open access, and service to community. While those things remain integral to their mission, community colleges have undergone a sea of change within the last decade, shifting their institutional focus from providing access alone to ensuring access with measurable and improved student success rates. Much of this progress has been driven by the work of leading foundations, such as Lumina Foundation, Bill & Melinda Gates Foundation, and Kresge Foundation, coupled with the impact of an overarching "completion agenda" that catalyzed what many consider the most significant reform movement in the history of community colleges.

The work of the *New Directions* authors and publishers reflects that spirit of reform. Through thoughtful and informed analysis of and potential solutions to such problems as the failure of developmental education as currently delivered, disappointing student completion rates, misalignment of curricula, and resultant competency gaps, the authors further advance understanding among community college practitioners and stakeholders. They also illuminate promising methodologies, such as "tuning," used to positive effect among European Union countries to harmonize degrees across disparate organizations by creating clear pathways and agreed-upon learning outcomes at every degree level.

Many of the ideas examined by *New Directions* authors correspond to the thinking and recommendations of the 21st Century Commission on the Future of Community Colleges, a blue-ribbon panel of national thought leaders convened by the American Association of Community Colleges (AACC) in 2011. Following release of the commission's report in April of 2012, AACC initiated an intensive implementation phase designed to provide scalable, actionable strategies to address the commission's seven key recommendations. Results from that effort will be included in a summary publication, provide dynamic content for a new virtual center, and be used to further engage community colleges and stakeholders nationwide. Still other insights from chapter authors reflect the collective experiences and forward thinking of Achieving the Dream leadership and data coaches who have spent close to a decade studying the elements needed for institutional transformation, now being implemented at close to 200 community colleges in 34 states.

What has been studied and is now shared by these authors has relevance across the campus leadership spectrum—administration, faculty, and support professionals. Some issues presented remain stubbornly persistent: the unmet need for financial aid and the unintended barriers to student completion. One author's observation relating to the issue of common core standards favored by state policymakers could well apply generally to what we all acknowledge is the very hard work ahead. There is no "silver bullet" to help meet urgent educational challenges. But while there is no silver bullet, there is, I am confident, a "silver lining" as we move forward. That optimism is inspired by the unquestioned commitment on the part of community college leaders imbued with a growing body of knowledge such as that found in *New Directions*.

WALTER G. BUMPHUS *is the president and CEO of American Association of Community Colleges.*

NEW DIRECTIONS FOR COMMUNITY COLLEGES • DOI: 10.1002/cc

*This chapter describes a movement to significantly increase student
attainment in community and technical colleges. The observations
of Leadership Coaches in Achieving the Dream, developed over a
nine-year period of involvement, provide insight into the leadership
required to transform institutional culture.*

Leadership Matters: Addressing the Student Success and Completion Agenda

Byron N. McClenney

There has been an enormous shift from a focus on access to one on student success in the community and technical college world during the past
decade. Even though the topics of productivity, accountability, and institutional effectiveness had surfaced during the previous two decades, nothing
like the student success and completion agenda has ever been observed in
over a century of experience in this sector of higher education. The work
on accountability and effectiveness (McClenney, 1997) had documented the
need for greater attention to student learning outcomes and attainment and
paved the way for a new movement on student success. It is the contention
here that Lumina Foundation for Education became a catalyst for the new
movement with the development of Achieving the Dream (ATD) during
2003–2004. They have since been joined by numerous foundations, think
tanks, and professional associations to create a national movement focused
on completion and student success. Achieving the Dream itself has now
reached almost 200 institutions in 34 states to form the most significant
reform movement in the history of community and technical colleges.

This author suggested in a Lumina-requested concept paper
(McClenney, 2003) that nothing short of institutional transformation
would be required to move the needle on student success. It was also
suggested that longitudinal or cohort tracking of all first-time students
would need to be at the heart of the transformational effort. Finally, it was
suggested that sound strategic thinking, relentlessly focused institutional
activity, and resources allocated in alignment with a focus on student
success would be required to get beyond the typical project mentality
observed in many community and technical colleges. With input from

NEW DIRECTIONS FOR COMMUNITY COLLEGES, no. 164, Winter 2013 © 2014 Wiley Periodicals, Inc.
Published online in Wiley Online Library (wileyonlinelibrary.com) • DOI: 10.1002/cc.20076

dozens of leaders in the field, Lumina made the decision to develop and then launch Achieving the Dream in 2004 in a cooperative venture with seven national partners (http://achievingthedream.org/).

Beginning of a Movement

The movement was launched in 2004 when 27 colleges came together in a kickoff to discuss how to create a culture of inquiry and evidence in pursuit of a transformational agenda. College teams were encouraged to develop a plan of action, which followed five important guiding principles: (a) committed leadership; (b) use of evidence to improve programs and services; (c) broad engagement of faculty, staff, governing boards, and community; (d) systemic institutional improvement; and (e) equity (added several years into the initiative).

All participating colleges pledged intensive work to increase the percentage of students who (a) complete the courses they take, earning a grade of C or higher; (b) complete developmental courses and move on to college-level courses; (c) enroll in and complete gatekeeper/gateway courses, such as introductory math and English; (d) re-enroll from one term to the next (persistence); and (e) earn certificates and degrees.

Disaggregation of these data on the basis of race, ethnicity, gender, and age became standard in the implementation of Achieving the Dream. This approach to the use of data has now become almost routine in numerous national efforts to focus the field on outcomes. An example is the Voluntary Framework of Accountability (VFA) emerging from the American Association of Community Colleges (AACC) in 2013.

Coaching for Transformation

Beginning with the 27 institutions in 2004, ATD colleges have been assisted by a Leadership Coach and a Data Coach who make multiday visits to the colleges, and who also work with the college teams during major learning events such as DREAM. The 44 Leadership Coaches who have been involved since 2004 have all worked for the Community College Leadership Program (CCLP) at The University of Texas at Austin, which was one of seven founding partners in the creation of the initiative. The collective experience of the Leadership Coaches, drawn from over 1,600 site visit reports and annual reflective retreats, provides more than has ever been known about what it takes to transform colleges including the major barriers and challenges to transformation. The work of John Kotter (1998) at Harvard was extremely helpful in framing the approach to the work. This collective experience is significantly augmented by the collective experience of the Data Coaches who meet regularly with Leadership Coaches in reflective retreats. These Data Coaches, working for Achieving the Dream, Inc., are vital team members in work with the colleges. Not surprising is the agreement reached by those two groups that leadership, including boards and faculty, and a pervasive culture of inquiry and evidence are the leading reasons for progress on a transformative college agenda where that has been observed.

The Role of Boards

A companion effort growing out of ATD has been the development of trustee training to support the student success and completion agenda. Houston Endowment, one of the early major funders of ATD, had an interest in the critical role of boards in the improvement of outcomes for students. That interest led to the creation of the Board of Trustees Institute (BOTI) for Texas colleges funded by the Endowment to be involved in ATD. The CCLP delivered the first event in 2007. The Greater Texas Foundation later joined this effort to expand the offering to more Texas colleges involved in 2013. A total of 28 boards have been involved in these institutes. The efforts in Texas led to a partnership between the Association of Community College Trustees (ACCT) and the CCLP to expand the institute idea. Funded by the Bill and Melinda Gates Foundation, these institutes have now been delivered in Ohio, Washington, Texas, Nebraska, and New Jersey. The list will expand during 2013–2014 to move the student success and completion agenda. Out of 23 events since 2007, the CCLP is now in a good position to talk about how boards can appropriately be involved in support of a chief executive who wants to move the agenda. The experience in the institutes and the reflections of leadership coaches come together in the ACCT publication (McClenney & Mathis, 2011) on the importance of the board role in support of a student success and completion agenda.

Individual college data are developed for each trustee event so that board members can understand the stakes involved. An example from multiple events might be helpful in understanding the approach. Cohort data are developed to follow all student testing into developmental education. If one follows all student testing into developmental math to see how many of these students complete a college-level math course in two years, then it is easy to understand the shock resulting from a single-digit percentage which is not unusual for most colleges. Board members can then begin to understand the challenge faced by a CEO who wants to improve the outcomes.

Effective Boards

From individual college site visit reports which comment on board actions and support to the interactions with board members at institutes, it is now possible to identify how boards can effectively support the student success agenda. Fundamental to progress is the key insight that boards must create the culture within which a CEO can engage the institution in courageous conversations about the data on student success. They realize their role to support the creation of a culture of inquiry and evidence by engaging in regular conversations about progress of students through the institution. They see the value of creating a strategic plan with student success at the core and the importance of approving goals for student success and equity. Monitoring key performance indicators such as those mentioned earlier can be seen as routine board agenda items. They begin to see how planning and budget allocations become tools to enhance the student success agenda. Data-informed conversations can be seen as early steps toward new policies to enhance outcomes. Whether or not to stop late registration, to mandate assessment and placement, to require orientation for all new students, or to create a student success course for all first-time students can be seen as building blocks in a cohesive student success agenda. "How do we know" and "Show me the data" can become acceptable responses when board members begin to see how to support the agenda. It becomes routine for board members to ask tough questions about progress on student success and completion.

Reasons for Progress

With a board commitment to student success, it becomes possible for a chief executive to exercise leadership for a student success and completion agenda. Not unexpected is the belief held by Leadership Coaches that leadership is the most critical. Data Coaches quickly add the culture of inquiry and evidence. In the best of circumstances, boards can create the culture within which a chief executive can lead courageous conversations leading to transformational actions. Coaches observe that a college is unable to have a full discussion of student success without cohort tracking of students and the use of disaggregated data.

When college leaders, supported by boards, begin to lead a process to look at student progression through the college, it becomes possible to identify gaps in outcomes on the basis of race, ethnicity, gender, age, and Pell Grant status. It becomes obvious that, in many colleges, more than 50% of all first-time college students are not college ready when they arrive on campus. That realization often leads to a review of student progression through developmental courses (basic skills, pre-collegiate, transitional, preparatory, remedial, and foundational are terms also used) as mentioned earlier in the mathematics example. Unfortunately, most institutions find students of color are disproportionately represented in developmental courses where they also have lower rates of success.

Inventory of Policies and Practices

As colleges begin to see the picture presented by the cohort data, coaches then frequently encourage colleges to take an inventory of policies and practices. Does late registration lead to lower outcomes? Does participation in orientation lead to better outcomes? Do all students go through assessment? Is placement following assessment a required next step? Do all students see an advisor before registration? Must students immediately enroll in developmental courses if assessment indicates the need? What courses produce the highest failure rates? In how many courses are 75% of the students enrolled (frequently no more than 25 courses out of an inventory of hundreds)? Answers to questions like these will typically lead to additional questions as an institution learns how to advance the agenda. Once the process is underway, it becomes possible to move beyond the notion that students have the right to fail and to focus instead on how to alter the college to make it possible for more to succeed. The seminal work of George Kuh (Kuh, Kinzie, Schuh, & Whitt, 2005) provides a useful frame within which to understand the transformative process.

Transformative Culture

The ATD coaches are very clear about what they observe in the colleges seen as moving the student success agenda. In addition to leadership and a culture of evidence, they frequently talk about a sustained focus on student success demonstrably influencing the development of policies, procedures, and practices. When talking about barriers and challenges, they frequently mention how overload and competing priorities contribute to the inability to sustain the focus over a long period.

Movement to create a shared vision followed by collaborative work to advance the agenda will be cited as critical in developing a strategy for broad and continuous faculty and staff engagement. Many colleges use convocations, data summits, town hall meetings, student focus groups, and strategic planning events to foster involvement and engagement in the student success work. Faculty and staff leadership will emerge when the culture of the institution encourages people to confront the tough issues. In discussion of challenges, coaches describe many ways people work to avoid the tough issues. They coach for shared ownership of problems as a way to pave the way for shared responsibility.

Virtually, all of the colleges seen as making progress appear to have effective processes for planning and budgeting. The processes are aligned with the vision, priorities, and strategies of a student success agenda. Most of the colleges are beginning to realize the power in the reallocation of existing resources. Resources are viewed broadly and include money, personnel, time, and space. Student success at the core of a strategic plan, a limited number of priorities driving budget development, and significant reallocation of resources can propel a college through a transformative process. When coaches stop to consider the barriers or challenges to transformation, they frequently cite competing priorities or the failure to sustain focus over a long period. An effective planning process with broad engagement can provide the discipline through which critical issues are identified and decisions about what is most important can be made. Courageous conversations are frequently documented along the way.

Another characteristic frequently observed is the process of integrating other significant initiatives into the systemic student success agenda. Effective planning facilitates this process. The quality improvement aspects of accreditation, strategic planning, work on student learning outcomes, grant programs such as Title III and Title V, and many other initiatives are seen as parts of a cohesive student success agenda. The integrated agenda can help overcome another frequently cited barrier which is simply overload. When people see a clear, focused agenda, they are enabled to work with more efficiency and effectiveness. They can see the possibility of moving beyond what is often called resistance to change to become collaborators in managing necessary change.

When the potential for a shared vision begins to emerge, it becomes possible to communicate a sense of urgency on campus and in the community. Board agendas look different, cabinet and faculty senate agendas begin to change, themes for convocations reinforce the urgency to transform processes, and community meetings can become venues for a different conversation about what is at stake.

The notion of managing change leads to the importance of professional development for all involved. The colleges seen as making progress pay attention to the emerging importance of professional development, particularly as it impacts adjunct faculty. In tight financial times, it is unlikely that colleges will be adding significant numbers of full-time faculty. A strategy to engage adjunct faculty in transformational processes and in changing instructional policies and practices becomes critical. Full-time faculty need help in defining and assessing learning outcomes and on course redesign. Deans and department heads need help in fostering different approaches to learning and in spreading promising interventions to serve larger numbers of students. The colleges on the path to transformation are paying attention to these needs. They are also focused on the front door of the college where front line staff create the first impressions and the first connections for incoming students. Robust professional development efforts in the most effective colleges are engaging all personnel in a cohesive program to support student success. Intentional design efforts are supported and silos are broken along the way.

A final major observation about colleges making progress deals with the way policies and practices are examined and revised to support the student success agenda. Colleges, as a result of data review, will typically then do an inventory of policies and practices in light of new understandings about how students progress through the institution. Most institutions discovered through learning events and coaching visits the emerging idea that much more should be mandated at the point of entry to the college. They also discovered they were not alone in needing to focus on the redesign of developmental education programs. In both cases, as well in the development of strategies to engage all faculty, the colleges began to develop interventions informed by and adapted from demonstrably effective practices.

Colleges experiencing the shifts described in the "Reasons for Progress" were beginning to see a shift in culture. This altered culture is one in which new ideas can be tested, new policies can be implemented, and interventions can be piloted, evaluated, and scaled-up to serve large numbers of students.

Changes at the Front Door

Many colleges started their work with a debate over whether or not to stop late registration. When access was the focus, it could be argued that it made sense to continue to register students until a census date. With success as the focus, it could be argued that it made no sense to admit students after a class held its first meeting.

When the notion that students have the right to fail held sway, it did not seem necessary to cause all students to go through an assessment and placement process. Colleges are now realizing the importance of assessment and the impact of the high stakes that go with assessment. Many now mandate a refresher before assessment, and some are creating a multiweek bridge program or "boot camp" to help students avoid the need for developmental courses or to at least place at a higher level.

Proper placement following assessment is emerging as a priority for many colleges. The importance of advising for all is increasingly being viewed as a critical element upfront.

Many colleges are now mandating orientation for all first-time enrollees which had not been the practice in the past. Some of these colleges are beginning to cluster students by interest areas like STEM, health careers, business, and liberal arts so that students begin to make connections with other students with similar interests during the orientation process.

Students who are not fully college ready are now being directed in their first term into developmental experiences leading to college readiness. A companion mandate for a first-term student success course has emerged as a way to be sure students learn how to "do college" and to help them create a mandated educational plan or pathway no later than the end of the first term of enrollment.

This shift in colleges beginning to move the needle on success has reduced the options for entering students. Efforts are being made to show students a pathway to success and to help them make early connections with other students as well as faculty and staff. This work reinforces and augments the formative work described by Barefoot et al. (2005).

Promising Interventions

Coaches work hard with their colleges to avoid jumping to interventions before the comprehensive review of data about progression through the college. They encourage a review or inventory of policies and practices, and coach for broad engagement in courageous conversations about student success. Efforts are made to identify achievement gaps on the basis of race, ethnicity, gender, age, or family income. Questions are raised about the success of current efforts to improve outcomes, and college teams are encouraged to do a review of the literature in the field. Once these steps have been taken, it becomes possible to thoughtfully explore interventions with the potential to help more students be successful.

An early pattern was for colleges to do pilots before scaling to large numbers. The evaluation of a pilot frequently led to a scaled-up version or to a decision to drop the intervention, or at least to revise and refine before scaling. In later years, some colleges have begun work at scale if they felt they found enough evidence of success in other ATD colleges. A new report, drawing from practices in numerous ATD colleges and others, describes high-impact practices (Center for Community College Student Engagement, 2013) with promise.

The reviews previously described frequently led to the realization that lack of student success in mathematics needed to lead to a priority for redesign of courses and methodology. Significant work is now underway to create new pathways to and through a college credit math course. Statistics, quantitative reasoning, and STEM-related pathways have emerged as promising. Creation of modules, hybrid approaches, emporiums or open-entry and open-exit labs, and various models of fast-track offerings are being tested around the ATD network.

Many colleges are working to combine developmental writing and developmental reading into a Developmental English model. Others are beginning to require learning lab participation (some for extra credit) for at least those falling below a "C" in a course.

Collaborative or cooperative learning approaches are emerging as the big bet for some colleges as they seek to engage faculty in all disciplines. Students in focus groups are very supportive of this approach to engagement.

Supplemental instruction or learning has been a choice by many as a way to support struggling students. The model includes involvement of a student who previously passed a course, who works with a faculty member in class and then conducts a supplemental session outside the scheduled class.

Learning communities, involving linked courses and advisors, allow faculty members to create a cohort experience for students and are showing promise in some colleges. A few colleges are making this intervention their big bet, particularly for developmental offerings.

Technology is enabling many colleges to start early alert programs so that students are directed to an intervention when they begin to falter. Case managers or student success coaches may be the ones to intervene after a referral is made by a faculty member.

Coaches report positive results on these interventions across multiple institutions, but they also report on the difficulty of taking them to scale. When asked in one of the regular meetings of coaches, they were, however, able to cite successful efforts in developmental programs to reach most or all of the students who might benefit. Most frequently cited efforts were student success courses with intrusive advising, developmental math redesign, and mandatory orientation which they have begun to describe as high-impact practices. These experiences provide reinforcement for previous research (Moore & Shulock, 2009) and reviews (Pascarella & Terenzini, 2005) focused on persistence and student success.

A Movement

What started as an idea in 2003 has become a movement involving approximately 200 colleges in 34 states. The movement has altered the national conversation and led to a national imperative to significantly increase student attainment. Colleges have learned how to change institutional culture to create the focus on student success. Leaders have led courageous conversations and engaged faculty and staff to examine progression of students through their colleges. Out of a culture of inquiry and evidence, ATD coaches have observed successful interventions being tested, evaluated, and then scaled-up to larger numbers of students. The Community College Research Center (Bailey, Jaggars, & Jenkins, 2011), an original partner in ATD, has created a particularly helpful site for a review on the research of interventions. While observing that this is no "silver bullet" and that scaling is difficult, coaches are beginning to describe high-impact practices with promise. The characteristics of a transformed culture have been described, and leadership has been affirmed as the most important element in the work. That leadership can be exercised most effectively when boards establish a priority for student success and create the culture within which leaders can do courageous work.

References

Bailey, T., Jaggars, S. S., & Jenkins, D. (2011, January). *Effective practices research conducted by Community College Research Center (CCRC) with support from the Bill and Melinda Gates Foundation.* Retrieved from http://ccrc.tc.columbia.edu /publications/introduction-assessment-of-evidence.html

Barefoot, B., Gardner, J., Cutright, M., Morris, L., Schroeder, C., Schwartz, S., & Swing, R. (2005). *Achieving and sustaining institutional excellence for the first year of college.* San Francisco, CA: Jossey-Bass.

Center for Community College Student Engagement. (2013). *A matter of degrees: Engaging practices, engaging students (High-impact practices for community college engagement)*. Austin: The University of Texas at Austin, Community College Leadership Program.

Kotter, J. P. (1998). Leading change: Why transformation efforts fail. In J. Collins & J. I. Porras (Eds.), *Harvard business review on change* (pp. 1–20). Boston, MA: Harvard Business School Publishing.

Kuh, G., Kinzie, J., Schuh, J., & Whitt, E. (2005). *Student success in college: Creating conditions that matter*. San Francisco, CA: AAHE and Jossey-Bass.

McClenney, B. (1997). Creating a climate for learning. In T. O'Banion (Ed.), *A learning college for the 21st century* (pp. 211–224). Washington, DC: American Council on Education.

McClenney, B. (2003). *Internal concept paper for the Lumina Foundation*. Unpublished.

McClenney, B., & Mathis, M. (2011). *Making good on the promise of the open door*. Washington, DC: Association of Community College Trustees.

Moore, C., & Shulock, N. (2009). *Student progress toward degree completion: Lessons from the research literature*. Sacramento, CA: Institute for Higher Education Policy.

Pascarella, E. T., & Terenzini, P. T. (2005). *How college affects students: A third decade of research* (Vol. 2). San Francisco, CA: Jossey-Bass.

BYRON N. MCCLENNEY *is the director of Student Success Initiatives in the program of higher education leadership at The University of Texas at Austin. He is also the national director of leadership coaching for Achieving the Dream.*

2

The completion agenda is in full force at the nation's community colleges. To maximize the impact colleges can have on improving completion, colleges must organize around using student progress and outcome data to monitor and track their efforts. Unfortunately, colleges are struggling to identify relevant data and to mobilize staff to review student information that can lead to action: changes in policy and practice that improve student completion. The authors present their model for engaging educational institutions in using data to make good decisions about increasing completion.

Maximizing Data Use: A Focus on the Completion Agenda

Brad C. Phillips, Jordan E. Horowitz

Educational institutions nationally are struggling with issues related to data. There is an abundance of data, but turning it into information that can be used remains elusive. To make use of data for improving student outcomes—including advancing the College Completion Agenda—community colleges, individually and collectively, should be asking:

- What metrics are valuable?
- How does a college organize around using data in a positive, nonthreatening way?
- What can leadership do to set the stage for motivating staff to engage around using data to inform policy and influence practice?

These and other questions set up a number of challenges for community colleges when engaging staff around data. Challenges include the sheer number of indicators, bringing data use to the fore, engaging faculty and staff, and encouraging data use across the institution.

Data, Indicators, and Metrics

Part of the challenge of encouraging data use for continuous program improvement is the sheer number of indicators, all seeming equally weighted

New Directions for Community Colleges, no. 164, Winter 2013 © 2014 Wiley Periodicals, Inc.
Published online in Wiley Online Library (wileyonlinelibrary.com) • DOI: 10.1002/cc.20077

in their importance. They include metrics collected nationally, within a state, and within an institution. These data typically are reported for accountability purposes. Typically, these data are not fed back to administrators, faculty, and staff throughout the college to be used in support of institutional decision making and assessment of program and practice changes.

For example, IPEDS is a national data collection system used by all institutions, but rarely do these institutions use their submitted data to inform their own policy and practice. Like most educational data, IPEDS is treated as a one-way street designed to satisfy reporting and accountability requirements when, in fact, the data are rich with information about student persistence and progress to degrees. Other large-scale data collection efforts include the Voluntary Framework for Accountability (VFA) Complete College America (CCA), the national benchmarking project, and others that hold information, such as student persistence, movement out of remediation, and successful transfers to four-year institutions. Colleges are also engaged in state-wide collection and reporting systems, usually associated with accountability and performance funding decisions. Locally data are collected and reported for program review, accreditation, master planning, and other administrative efforts.

The data source is not as important as timing and relevance. In fact, multiple sources of data can help paint a complete picture of the student experience. Policy makers and practitioners care about receiving the right data at the right time to make the best decision possible. Data inform decision making, help to monitor progress over time, reduce uncertainty about the potential future, and expand our thinking. Too often, though, the data are not available, do not address the problem adequately, or are in an unusable form. Community college administrators, faculty, and staff do not receive relevant data in a timely manner, which makes the information obsolete and useless.

Staff care about data that are relevant to them based on what they can influence. Talking to faculty about statewide completion rates is far removed from student completion and retention in their classroom. Yet, the two metrics are related. If students are not retained in the semester and not earning a successful course grade, they are not moving toward completion. Hence, it is important to provide information to faculty about what they can influence with their practice and make the link for them to broader institutional policy concerns obvious.

A Model for Improving Data Use in Colleges

To help colleges make better use of metrics at multiple levels and from multiple sources, the Institute for Evidence-Based Change (IEBC) developed a model for improving data use. IEBC works with community colleges to identify metrics important to their institution at multiple levels (faculty, president, chief financial officers, student services, and so on), identify the data required to track these metrics, and create systems to ensure the data are collected internally and externally. IEBC then provides professional development to community college administrators and lead faculty to ensure the data are presented as useful and usable information, which means it is timely and relevant. Finally, we work with community colleges to develop organizational habits that ensure the institution integrates data use in a systematic and systemic way that leads to a sustainable culture of evidence-driven decision making and continuous program improvement.

If a college is serious about making improvements in student success and completion, they cannot rely on current practices around data use. The IEBC model is a three-legged stool supporting effective use of data: analytics, human judgment and behavior, and organizational habits. Analytics includes data collection efforts, data storage, and accessibility. Human judgment and behavior takes into account how human beings perceive and process information, and how we make decisions based on that information. This area incorporates the latest information on neuroscience and behavioral economics. Finally, organizational habits address how leaders can build data use into the everyday workings of a community college.

Analytics

Our experience indicates that most colleges undervalue data collection, analysis, and reporting. In community colleges data are generally poorly managed. Yet, data have the potential to realize great benefits, but only if managed and used properly (Redman, 2008). Colleges tend to be very proficient at managing staff, buildings, and funds. Yet staff leave, buildings decay, and funds vary by budget cycles and legislative prerogative. Data collection, analysis, and reporting are some of the few things in a community college environment that can be controlled.

Data Collection.   Data collection must be conducted in a scientifically rigorous manner. This means paying attention to the quality of the data—ensuring what is collected accurately represents the population to which it refers. As one state education department report eloquently stated, "The data are error-free, however we cannot ensure the accuracy" (A. Macdonald, personal communication, March 29, 2013). The first step to ensuring scientifically rigorous data is to validate the format of what is being reported. It is easy to develop and run a validation program to ensure date fields contain dates or that codes used in data fields are within range. However, this is not done systematically or systemically, which results in errors such as social security numbers with upper case letter O used instead of the numeric zero.

More difficult, perhaps, is ensuring the accuracy of the data in the system—the data's validity. That is, to what extent does the data in the system accurately represent the educational institution's reality? Poor validity checks are related to resource issues. Large college systems cannot check a sample of data records large enough to make a difference. Small colleges tend to be under-resourced and do not have the capacity or knowledgeable staff to do so. One solution is to improve the accuracy of the data being entered.

How data get into the system is critical. It requires consistent data entry, and we strongly recommend a data entry audit. This is a process that ensures consistency every time data are entered into a system, no matter the site or form (electronic or paper-based). The stems (questions) and response sets (answers) in the data entry system must match the forms from which they are taken: using the same order and using the exact same language. Too often data entry sites vary from the data source, and there is little consistency from one data entry system to another within institutions—from financial aid to student services, for example.

The lack of continuity when an educational institution invests in a new data system also contributes to poor data quality. Colleges must insist that vendors link current data systems with the new system. Check to be sure this is not excluded in the work order.

Finally, using data for myriad purposes improves data quality. More people looking at the data will expose poor data: "This doesn't match the report we got last year" or "These aren't the students who were registered for my class." Instead of throwing up our hands and accepting that this is what was, is, and always will be, we need to push for improved data quality. We cannot accurately track student outcomes, including completion, if we are using information that cannot be trusted. Furthermore, we cannot improve student outcomes if we do not have reliable and valid data to accurately assess why students are not achieving to desired levels.

Analysis.   Simple analyses of information, frequencies, and percentages disaggregated by subpopulations of interest (ethnicity, gender, special needs populations, and so on) generally meet the needs of college faculty and administrators. Sophisticated analyses are rarely necessary. One exception could be for institutions using predictive analytics, but these institutions are few and far between. A single number displaying student course success rates is often the best motivator to have the courageous conversation needed to improve student outcomes.

Trend data are critically important and rarely examined. There are two ways of analyzing trend data, and they serve different purposes. First is to identify a single cohort of students, say those entering in a specified term and tracking them over time. This is useful for understanding how students progress through a college or program in a college. The second way is to compare students in a program or college year after year. This is helpful to understand the impact of innovations and interventions on student progress.

Reporting.   If a college is going to change its culture around data use, then data must be available to all staff. Data must be accessible to be usable and usable to be useful. The keys to the castle cannot only be held by the institutional research or information technology office. Changing culture around data use requires a college-wide effort to engage all staff talking about student outcomes around the water cooler.

If the culture of a college is going to change around the use of data, it must be made available to all staff at the time they need it. There are several providers of web-based dashboards and business intelligence tools that, if carefully constructed and deployed, can be accessed easily and understood at a glance. Gone are the days of data in the form of *green-bar* paper. Unfortunately, too many colleges try to provide the information from full reports with a dashboard. But the rule of *less is more* is appropriate. If staff are to focus on what's important, easily available data need to be explicit and brief. Too often staff are confronted with displays and reports that display myriad data metrics and they do not know which data are important. Some rules of data presentation are keep it simple, less is more, and use pictures to describe a phenomenon rather than numbers. Charts are often, but not always, better than tables. We like to use the rule that any piece of data that is reported needs to be understood by T. C. Mits and T. C. Wits—The Celebrated Man (and Woman) In The Street (Lieber, 1944).

Finally, it is important that colleges focus on leading and lagging indicators. According to McChesney, Covey, and Huling (2012), leading indicators are those that a college has control over and can influence the lagging indicators. For example, the rate at which a cohort of first time in college students earns a degree or certificate is a lagging indicator. Course completion is a leading indicator: it relates to the lagging indicator, completion, and can be influenced by a variety of actions taken by faculty, academic counselors, and others. By focusing on the leading indicators, staff feel empowered to engage in what they can control. Leading indicators include metrics, such as course completion rates, course grades, and retention within the term. Lagging indicators include persistence from term to term, degree attainment, transfer to four-year institutions, and employment and wage data.

New work is emerging in predictive analytics. That is, collecting data on a large number of variables, which are entered into a modeling formula that can provide a prediction of a student's course success and subsequent completion. These tools are becoming ever more sophisticated. Although we might believe that as veteran staff our predictions about a student's possibility of success are likely, statistical formulas have been shown to provide much greater accuracy.

Human Judgment and Behavior

The IEBC model takes into account recent research about human judgment and behavior. We now know a great deal about how we make decisions and the relationships among data, emotions, and decision making. We apply this knowledge to improve the chances that community college administrators, faculty, and staff can and will make use of the data provided to them.

Presentation Is a Key Element.   When presenting any data, it is important to link that data to the story of an individual student or a group of students. Creating an emotional connection to a data point helps people engage more in the information. Creating this link also puts a picture in the head of the staff member. They can view the information not only clinically but also emotionally, helping them to better focus on the problem to be solved.

Often data are presented in the format of *here it is*, thus allowing no connection to the issue. It is best to begin any data presentation with a description of the problem and then providing data to support that description. Human beings are problem solvers. By presenting the data in support of a problem to be solved, greater focus is achieved by staff members on working to understand the extent of the problem and subsequent decisions to achieve a solution.

If data are complicated and difficult to understand, or too many data points are presented, we employ a different system of analysis and become more critical. We like things simple. If we have to work at getting the information we need, understand a chart or a table, the battle to communicate is lost. Human beings are looking to expend as little effort, or work through as little resistance, as possible. We are lazy by nature. Consequently, data presentations need to focus on one issue. Too many data points in one figure complicate comprehension, which leads to frustration and decreased attention.

Known as the framing effect (Kahneman, 2011), how information is presented is critical. If we say that a food is 90% fat free it is far more palatable than saying 10% fat. If a point about a problem needs to be highlighted, then it is best to say 33% of students were not successful in a course versus saying we have a 66% success rate. That said, when presenting information that is not positive one has to be careful not to threaten the receiver's self-esteem (or their job) as this could lead to resistance to engaging with the data. Data need to be presented with adequate time to discuss the implications. There is nothing worse in a data presentation to present horrific data about student performance with no opportunity to discuss ways to improve.

Getting to Decision Making.   Colleges sometimes struggle with making decisions about changes to policy and practice. This occurs even if we believe that the changes to be made will result in improved completion rates for our students. Research has shown that we have far more regret if we initiate change and it does not go well than if we do not make a change and it did not go well—stasis and loss aversion is built in to our nature (Thaler & Sunstein, 2009). One way to combat this is to see where else those changes have been made and the effects of the change. While there is little room to discuss implementation here, suffice it to say that any new changes must be implemented with fidelity or they will likely fall flat and not meet the intended effects.

NEW DIRECTIONS FOR COMMUNITY COLLEGES • DOI: 10.1002/cc

Organizational Habits

Community colleges have a culture and routines that center around a long history of doing business. There is a cadence of activities that are based on tradition and practice. It is a challenge to incorporate new efforts into this organizational rhythm. As a result, attempts to create a culture of data use often start (and end) with an addition to current practice rather than integration.

A common response to criticisms related to poor use of data is for a community college to establish a data committee charged with examining student outcomes. This committee is often ad hoc and disconnected from other activities and committees, operating in isolation. There may be great fanfare when the committee begins, but over time committee membership dwindles and the influence the committee has on policy and practice is minimal.

IEBC recommends that to increase data use, a college needs to integrate data into existing structures and practices. These include governing board meetings, program review, curriculum committees, department meetings, and administrator meetings. Most effective is to start each meeting with a piece of data related to the agenda and posing thoughtful questions about the data. No more than one or two data points are displayed and discussed. Discussing multiple data points dilutes the discussion and creates a diffusion of responsibility among the staff. Integrating data into every agenda then becomes a habit. Staff know every meeting will begin with a discussion of data. This is a considerable step in changing culture about data use.

In addition, colleges that have used data as a hammer to punish rather than a tool to enlighten will experience resistance in an attempt to increase data use. Administrators have to inform their community about the purpose of data use and their actions must follow their words: data are used to inform and influence our work—not to punish. When an institution has made such a commitment and the actions that follow support that commitment, then trust can be built and data are viewed not with suspicion but as a resource.

Research on neuroscience indicates that when staff are in a good mood, they are more receptive to reviewing data—even if the data are troubling (Kahneman, 2011). Each meeting should start off with staff talking about how they personally contributed to student success. Never launch directly into a data discussion. Furthermore, the addition of food helps with cognitive processing, as we know that engaging in deep discussions around data requires more glucose and food helps with that production. The bottom line is that when staff feel strained or threatened they are more likely to be suspicious, or worse, withdrawn. It is important to have staff engaged in the task, so feed them and make them feel comfortable. According to Kahneman (2011), "Good mood and cognitive ease are the human equivalents of assessments of safety and familiarity" (p. 90).

Too often, meetings are held close to the end of the day when staff are tired. Leaders need to make sure that they hold meetings about data during times of the day when staff have energy and are not fatigued. We recommend that lunch meetings are a good way to engage staff. Breaking bread together is a human custom that goes back to our roots and helps to set a positive mood.

Finally to avoid the domination of one person in meetings, staff should be able to review data, then write down, and verbally provide a brief summary of their thoughts and position on the matter. This avoids the domination of those who often speak early and with authority and helps every voice to be heard.

Finally, people tend to be overly optimistic about the potential success of a proposed intervention. They overestimate the potential gains and underestimate the potential pitfalls. To avoid this optimism and to ensure that any changes in policy and practice are fully vetted, it is important to engage in a premortem exercise (Klein, 2003). When a decision is being made about moving forward with a policy or practice change, committee members are asked to imagine that they are a year or two in the future and the implementation has gone horribly wrong. Members describe what went wrong and why. This exercise gives all members a chance to address implementation issues that may not have been discussed or fully addressed.

Notes must be taken at each meeting. It is important to memorialize what has been said and, more importantly, agreed upon. Too often in education we rely on memory rather than documentation. Notes also provide a history for new members, and as staff go on and off committees, a history can be reviewed.

Summary

This chapter has focused on how colleges can better use data to inform their institution's work on the College Completion Agenda. Too many colleges fail to use data at all or use data to little effect. Analytics, human judgment and decision making, and organizational habits all contribute to ensuring data are useful to policy makers and practitioners. Without accurate and usable data, we cannot measure the extent to which we are reaching our goals for our students or understand what needs to be done to improve our efforts.

References

Kahneman, D. (2011). *Thinking, fast and slow.* New York, NY: Farrar, Straus, Giroux.
Klein, G. (2003). *The power of intuition.* New York, NY: Crown Business Publishing.
Lieber, L. (1944). *The education of T. C. Mits.* New York, NY: W.W. Norton.

McChesney, C., Covey, S., & Huling, J. (2012). *The 4 disciplines of execution: Achieving your wildly important goals.* New York, NY: Simon and Schuster.

Redman, T. C. (2008). *Data driven: Profiting from your most important business asset.* Boston, MA: Harvard Business Review Press.

Thaler, R., & Sunstein, C. R. (2009). *Nudge: Improving decisions about health, wealth and happiness.* New York, NY: Penguin.

BRAD C. PHILLIPS *is the president and CEO of the Institute for Evidence-Based Change and a data coach for Achieving the Dream.*

JORDAN E. HOROWITZ *is the vice president for Foundation Relations and Project Development with the Institute for Evidence-Based Change and formerly senior project director in Evaluation Research at WestEd.*

3

In this chapter, we describe efforts by growing number of colleges and universities to redesign academic programs and support services to create "guided pathways" designed to increase the rate at which students enter and complete a program of study.

Get With the Program ... and Finish It: Building Guided Pathways to Accelerate Student Completion

Davis Jenkins, Sung-Woo Cho

Many Choices, Little Guidance

In research charting the educational pathways and outcomes of community college students, we found that students who enter a program of study in their first year are much more likely to complete a credential or transfer successfully than are students who do not get into a program until the second year or later (Jenkins & Cho, 2012). This is perhaps not surprising. What is surprising is how little attention many community colleges pay to helping students get into and through programs of study.

Most community colleges offer a wide array of programs. Yet, colleges typically provide little guidance to help new students choose a program of study and develop a plan for completing it (Venezia, Bracco, & Nodine, 2010). This is so even though many if not most new students enroll in community colleges without clear goals for college and careers and may not have a clear idea even of what the opportunities are (Gardenhire-Crooks, Collado, & Ray, 2006). Career services and advising are available to students who seek them out, but studies suggest that those who need them the most are least likely to take advantage of them (Karp, O'Gara, & Hughes, 2008).

Students who are undecided about what program to enter are often assigned to "general education" by default (Grubb, 2006). One rationale for treating undecided students as "general studies" students is that it gives them the opportunity to take a variety of courses and explore different fields without limiting any future options. However, even in states that have policies guaranteeing transfer of a core general education curriculum, there is no guarantee that credits will be accepted for credit toward junior standing

NEW DIRECTIONS FOR COMMUNITY COLLEGES, no. 164, Winter 2013 © 2014 Wiley Periodicals, Inc.
Published online in Wiley Online Library (wileyonlinelibrary.com) • DOI: 10.1002/cc.20078

in a particular major because major requirements are often set by individual departments within transfer destination institutions (Gross & Goldhaber, 2009). Thus, to guarantee efficient transfer of credits, students have to have a clear idea of what program they want to transfer to. And even if their goals are clear, information on transfer requirements is often complicated, hard to find, and unreliable (Kadlec & Martinez, 2013).

While community college departments closely monitor enrollment in their courses, they often do not know which students are pursuing programs of study in their fields and thus do not track students in their programs to ensure that they make steady progress toward achieving their goals for program completion and transfer (Karp, 2013). As a result, many students end up self-advising.

With so many choices and without a clear roadmap or someone monitoring their progress, it is not surprising that many community college students indicate that they are confused and often frustrated trying to find their way through college (Venezia et al., 2010). The lack of clear guidance can lead students to make costly decisions (Rosenbaum, Deil-Amen, & Person, 2006). Indeed, there is evidence from research on the course-taking patterns that many community college students are pursuing suboptimal pathways (Crosta, 2013). When asked, students indicate that being in a program with a well-defined pathway would improve their changes of persisting, completing, and transferring (Public Agenda, 2012).

Building Guided Pathways to Success

Under the prevailing model common to community colleges, students are left to navigate a complex and often confusing array of programs and courses and support services mostly on their own. Instead of letting students figure out their own paths through college, a growing number of colleges and universities are creating "guided pathways" for students. The elements of this approach include three key features, described as follows.

Clear Roadmaps to Student Goals. In institutions that have implemented guided pathways reforms, academic programs are clearly mapped out by faculty to create educationally coherent pathways, with learning outcomes clearly defined and aligned with the requirements for further education and, in occupational programs, for career advancement. Students are given a default sequence of courses to follow for their chosen programs based on maps created by faculty, although they can still opt out. Rather than restrict students' options, the guided pathways approach is intended to help them make better choices so that they will be more likely to achieve their goals.

On-Ramps to Programs of Study. Colleges and universities are rethinking intake, advising, and remediation as on-ramps to programs of study. Mechanisms are in place to help new students develop or clarify goals for college and careers and create an academic plan. As part of their plans, students are required to choose a field of study with a default curriculum that gives them a taste of the given field and helps them decide if they want to pursue a specialized course of study in the field or switch to another one. Teaching of academic foundation skills and college knowledge and success skills are contextualized in college-level coursework in the student's field of interest. Students who cannot be placed in college-level courses are helped to move through remediation as quickly as possible.

Embedded Advising, Progress Tracking, Feedback, and Support. Students' progress according to their plans is tracked and frequent feedback is provided to them, their advisors, and instructors. Advising is redesigned to ensure students are making progress based on academic and nonacademic milestones, such as choosing a major, applying for transfer, and updating a résumé. Close cooperation between professional advisors and faculty ensures smooth transition from initial general advising to advising in a program. Early-alert systems signal when students are struggling and set in motion appropriate support. Advising and other necessary supports are designed as defaults that students are expected to use unless they opt out.

Four-year institutions were among the pioneers in developing the guided pathways approach. One example is Florida State University (FSU), where, beginning in the late 1990s, faculty began developing program maps that lay out for every program default course sequences and milestones that students must achieve over the entire course of the program. Students who are undecided are required to choose an "exploratory major" in one of four fields. The exploratory majors give students a structured path for choosing a major. Students can only stay in a premajor for up to three terms, after which they have to choose a specific major. FSU has found that even with the guidance provided by the program maps and premajors, a robust system of advising and other supports is still needed, especially to help students select majors, for transfer students and other special populations, and for students who are not making progress or fall off-track. FSU officials contend that these efforts are at least part of the reason the university has been able to improve retention rates and graduation rates for students overall and for closing the graduation rate gap between minority students and their peers (Carey, 2008).

To help students choose from among the more than 250 majors it offers, Arizona State University (ASU) asked faculty members to map out the path to a degree in each field. They lay out a default curriculum for students to follow each semester and milestones students need to achieve to stay on track. They also identify "critical courses" that should be taken early in a student's program and can be used to predict a student's likely performance in the major. ASU uses a sophisticated electronic advising system called eAdvisor to monitor students' progress along their map and identify when they may be foundering. As at Florida State, undecided students are required to enter an exploratory major in one of the five most popular program areas. Like students in regular majors, students in exploratory majors are required to follow a "major map" which shows the prescribed sequence of courses by term. Students in exploratory majors are also required to enroll in a sequence of one-credit major and career exploration courses, which are designed to lead students through the process of choosing a major.

Based on the major maps, ASU has developed transfer admissions guarantees in particular majors with every community college in Arizona. Community college students who complete the sequence of courses specified in the agreement for a particular major are guaranteed admission as juniors into that major at ASU and receive a somewhat reduced level of tuition through ASU's Tuition Commitment Program (for Arizona residents). ASU is collaborating with the Maricopa Community Colleges and others to develop an information system to allow ASU and community advisors to track student progress along these pathways. ASU has also assigned transfer admissions specialists to work with students and their advisors on the community college campuses. This is an example of two- and four-year institutions working together to develop guided transfer pathways on a very large scale.

Community colleges are also beginning to implement the guided pathways approach on their own. In selecting Valencia College as the first winner of the Aspen Prize for Community College Excellence, the Aspen Institute cited Valencia's "life map" academic and career planning system that is linked to clear pathways, including "premajor" tracks aligned with the requirements for junior standing in majors at partner universities for students seeking to transfer.

In 2009, Queensborough Community College in New York began requiring all first-time, full-time students to enroll in one of five Freshmen Academies based on their interests and goals. Each academy has a "freshmen coordinator" who serves as an academic advisor and advocate for students in that academy, and at least one faculty coordinator responsible for working with faculty and student affairs staff to promote the adoption of high-impact teaching practices and build academic communities of students, faculty, and others with similar interests and aspirations. The college has surveyed students in the Academies extensively. According to the college researcher who oversees evaluation of the Academies, "Students say that being in an academy gives them a sense of identity as a student…. It causes them to reflect on what they want to do, and what it will take to move ahead in the field" (D. Jenkins, personal communication, May, 2013). Students are not locked into a particular Academy. The experience in an Academy leads some students to change their minds about what they want to study and do; indeed, approximately 20% of students switch academies in the first year. The college reports that after implementing the Freshman Academies in fall 2009, first-year retention rates increased. The college's three-year graduation rate for first-time, full-time students has also increased since then. College staff acknowledge that they cannot attribute these improvements to the Academies alone, pointing out the college has done many things during this period to improve student outcomes. Still, these results along with very positive reviews by students and faculty have convinced the college to require all new students, whether full or part time, to enroll in an Academy when they enter the college.

In examining why many of its students do not complete, Miami Dade College (MDC) found that the pathways to program completion were often unclear, particularly in the "pre-baccalaureate" program area, where the largest number of students are enrolled and where completion rates are also relatively low. Students had too many choices of courses. Academic support was often misaligned with academic programs, and the information students received to help them navigate programs and services was often inconsistent and unclear.

To address this, in academic year 2012–2013, MDC convened a group of 27 faculty members who, in consultation with their departments and college-wide instructional committees, mapped out program pathways in the five largest program areas, which account for over 80% of degree-seeking students at the college. The charge to the pathways mapping team was to create maps that specify a default sequence of courses for students pursuing degrees in those fields. The maps, which included versions for full- and part-time students, had to meet three criteria. First, all courses in each pathway must transfer seamlessly to enable students to achieve junior standing in target bachelor's programs. Second, each pathway should indicate specific general education courses that are relevant to the given major field. For example, the pathway map might say: "This is the social science course recommended for Criminal Justice majors." And third, the curriculum should provide opportunities for students to master all 10 MDC learning goals for general education.

All entering students are required to see an advisor and develop an academic plan based on the pathway maps. MDC is also creating "communities of interest," default first-year programs of study in broad fields like business or health science that will be designed to introduce students to the field and decide if they want to pursue more specialized study or switch to another field. Thus, rather than implement small innovations and try to scale them up, MDC, like the other institutions profiled here, is innovating at scale, redesigning programs and support services in ways that will affect thousands of students.

Supporting Evidence

Rigorous research on the effectiveness of guided pathways in higher education is just beginning. An example, in preliminary results from a random-assignment study of CUNY's Accelerated Study in Associate Programs (ASAP), which requires students to attend college full time in a block-scheduled course of study and provides a rich array of supports and incentives for up to three years, MDRC found extraordinarily strong effects on student retention and credit accumulation (Scrivener, Weiss, & Sommo, 2012).

Research on organizational effectiveness and improvement strongly suggests that to achieve large improvements in student outcomes, piecemeal changes will not suffice. Rather than try to bring to scale "best practices," colleges and universities need to redesign their policies, programs, and services at scale (Jenkins, 2011). The guided pathways approach reflects a set of principles of practice that are supported in the research literature and that colleges can follow in this redesign process. Three of these principles are described briefly as follows.

Defaults and Active Choice.   The complex processes students have to negotiate to enroll in and navigate through broad-access institutions can be overwhelming for students. A large body of rigorous research from behavioral psychology indicates that too many complex choices can lead to the sorts of behaviors we often see in students: indecision, procrastination, self-doubt, and paralysis (Thaler & Sunstein, 2008). In contrast, a simplified set of options including clear information on each option's costs and benefits, or the provision of a "default option" designed by experts, can each help people make more optimal decisions. Applied to broad-access institutions, the findings from this research suggest that colleges would achieve better outcomes by simplifying bureaucratic procedures (such as registering for classes and applying for financial aid) and offering more clearly structured programs, each with clearly defined and prescribed requirements, sequence of courses, and expected outcomes (Scott-Clayton, 2011). One reason that community colleges are so dependent on advisors is that the program paths are not clear and students need an expert to help navigate through the maze of choices students encounter. But because the current paths are often so complicated that even expert advisors sometimes cannot figure them out, they not only need to be clarified, they must be simplified as well.

Research on behavioral psychology shows that people can handle complex decisions if they are helped to think through the options hierarchically. One way to do this is by organizing complex choices into more manageable sets, but requiring the chooser to choose from among the sets (Keller, Harlam, Loewenstein, & Volpp, 2011). This "active choice" technique is apparent in the efforts described earlier of institutions like Arizona State to organize specific degree programs into a limited set of broad streams or exploratory majors that new students are required to select, but that help guide them through the process of choosing a specific major—or switching to another field if their initial choice is not a good fit.

Program Coherence.   Research on K–12 education finds that schools that are able to achieve greater gains in student outcomes, particularly with students from disadvantaged backgrounds, have higher levels of "instructional program coherence." This is defined as "a set of interrelated programs for students and staff that are guided by a common framework for curriculum, instruction, assessment, and learning climate, and that are pursued over a sustained period of time" (Newmann, Smith, Allensworth, & Bryk, 2001, p. 299). The programs and supports offered by community colleges are often lacking in coherence. By this principle, to improve student outcomes, colleges need to ensure that all aspects of their programs and services—including orientation and intake, placement testing, remediation, curriculum, instruction, assessment, academic support, and so on—are well integrated and aligned to achieve program-level learning goals.

Integrated Supports.   Research suggests that college students benefit from nonacademic supports that help them create social relationships, clarify goals for college and careers, develop college know-how, and address conflicting demands of work, family, and college. Efforts to build on-ramps that help students choose and enter a program of study should include supports that address these four areas (Karp, 2011). These support services should ideally be offered in a way that is integrated into students' primary academic experience rather than offered separately. Behavioral research and research on learning suggests that it is motivating for students to see how they are proceeding along their chosen path. Thus, it is critical to provide frequent feedback to students on how they are progressing, both to encourage students who have reached important milestones and to help students who are not making progress or who are off-track.

None of these principles suggests a single best way that colleges should carry out any of their many functions. Instead, they represent principles of practice, grounded in research, that colleges can follow in redesigning programs and supports to increase the rate at which students enter and complete a program of study.

Collaboration Is Key

Collaboration is important to any major organizational reform, but it is critical to efforts to implement guided pathways. To map out program pathways, faculty need to work with transfer institutions and employers in order to define meaningful learning outcomes. And they must also collaborate within and across departments to systematically build those outcomes across a clearly defined sequence of courses. To help guide students into those pathways and keep them on track, faculty and student services staff need to work together to monitor and support students as they enter and progress along a program path.

For guided pathways reforms to be successful, therefore, college leaders need to create time and support for faculty and staff to collaborate. As it is, professional development at community colleges is often viewed either as information sharing geared to a wide audience on campus—such as at the typical faculty development day—or an activity design to build the skills and knowledge of individual faculty members. Colleges might consider redirecting at least some resources currently spent on conventional forms of professional development to collaborative efforts, such as providing training, facilitation, and other support as needed by teams of faculty and staff working together to create guided pathways. This reframes professional development as a strategic activity that supports the collective involvement of faculty and staff in organizational improvement rather than an activity that mainly supports professional growth of faculty and staff as individuals.

To build an infrastructure that will support ongoing efforts to implement and improve guided pathways, colleges need to rethink not only their approach to professional development, but also their committee structures, institutional research activities, program review processes, budgeting practices, and policies for employee hiring, performance review, and incentives. All such practices should be reviewed with a view to ensuring that efforts to increase the rate at which students "get with a program...and finish it" become an integral part of the way community colleges do business.

References

Carey, K. (2008). *Graduation rate watch: Making minority student success a priority.* Washington, DC: Education Sector.

Crosta, P. (2013, April). *Intensity and attachment: How the chaotic enrollment patterns of community college students affect educational outcomes* (CCRC Working Paper No. 60). New York, NY: Columbia University, Teachers College, Community College Research Center.

Gardenhire-Crooks, A., Collado, H., & Ray, B. (2006). *A whole 'nother world: Students navigating community college.* New York, NY: MDRC.

Gross, B., & Goldhaber, D. (2009). *Community college transfer and articulation policies: Looking beneath the surface.* Seattle, WA: Center on Reinventing Public Education.

Grubb, W. N. (2006). "Like, what do I do now?": The dilemmas of guidance counseling. In T. Bailey & V. Morest (Eds.), *Defending the community college equity agenda* (pp. 195–222). Baltimore, MD: Johns Hopkins University Press.

Jenkins, D. (2011). *Redesigning community colleges for completion: Lessons from research on high-performance organizations* (CCRC Working Paper No. 24, Assessment of Evidence Series). New York, NY: Columbia University, Teachers College, Community College Research Center.

Jenkins, D., & Cho, S.-W. (2012). *Get with the program: Accelerating community college students' entry into and completion of programs of study* (CCRC Working Paper No. 32). New York, NY: Community College Research Center, Teachers College, Columbia University.

Kadlec, A., & Martinez, M. (2013, April 26). *Putting it all together: Strengthening pathways between comprehensives and community colleges.* Prepared for the American Enterprise Institute Private Convening, "Comprehending Comprehensives."

Karp, M. M. (2011, April). *Toward a new understanding of non-academic student support: Four mechanisms encouraging positive student outcomes in the community college* (CCRC Working Paper No. 28, Assessment of Evidence Series). New York, NY: Columbia University, Teachers College, Community College Research Center.

Karp, M. M. (2013). *Entering a program: Helping students make academic and career decisions* (CCRC Working Paper No. 59, Assessment of Evidence Series). New York, NY: Columbia University, Teachers College, Community College Research Center.

Karp, M. M., O'Gara, L., & Hughes, K. L. (2008). *Do support services at community colleges encourage success or reproduce disadvantage? An exploratory study of students in two community colleges* (CCRC Working Paper No. 10). New York, NY: Columbia University, Teachers College, Community College Research Center.

Keller, P. A., Harlam, B., Loewenstein, G., & Volpp, K. G. (2011). Enhanced active choice: A new method to motivate behavior change. *Journal of Consumer Psychology, 21*, 376–383.

Newmann, F. M., Smith, B., Allensworth, E., & Bryk, A. S. (2001). Instructional program coherence: What it is and why it should guide school improvement policy. *Educational Evaluation and Policy Analysis, 23*(4), 297–321.

Public Agenda. (2012). *Student voices on the higher education pathway: Preliminary insights and stakeholder engagement considerations.* San Francisco, CA: WestEd.

Rosenbaum, J. E., Deil-Amen, R., & Person, A. E. (2006). *After admission: From college access to college success.* New York, NY: Russell Sage Foundation.

Scott-Clayton, J. (2011). *The shapeless river: Does a lack of structure inhibit students' progress at community colleges?* (CCRC Working Paper No. 25, Assessment of Evidence Series). New York, NY: Columbia University, Teachers College, Community College Research Center.

Scrivener, S., Weiss, M. J., & Sommo, C. (2012). *What can a multifaceted program do for community college students? Early results from an evaluation of Accelerated Study in Associate Programs (ASAP) for developmental education students.* New York, NY: MDRC.

Thaler, R. H., & Sunstein, C. R. (2008). *Nudge: Improving decisions about health, wealth, and happiness.* New Haven, CT: Yale University Press.

Venezia, A., Bracco, K. R., & Nodine, T. (2010). *One-shot deal? Students' perceptions of assessment and course placement in California's community colleges.* San Francisco, CA: WestEd.

DAVIS JENKINS is a senior research associate at the Community College Research Center at Teachers College, Columbia University.

SUNG-WOO CHO is a quantitative research associate at the Community College Research Center at Teachers College, Columbia University.

The college completion agenda, in concert with recent research, has brought scrutiny to the shortcomings of community college remedial programs. Remedial, or developmental, education has come to be seen as a hindrance to student progress and attainment rather than as a support. In this chapter, the authors describe new approaches to help students prepare for and move into college-level courses more quickly, while cautioning that we do not know yet whether many of them are effective.

Acceleration Strategies in the New Developmental Education Landscape

Andrea Venezia, Katherine L. Hughes

Over the past decade, the policy priority for community colleges nationally shifted from a singular focus on preserving the open access mission to a dual emphasis on access and supporting student success. There is not a clear consensus about how to define success, given that students enroll in community colleges for disparate reasons, including to earn associate degrees, to complete certificate programs, to gain some credits before transferring to a four-year institution, and to take noncredit coursework. There is general agreement, however, that a large proportion of community college students leave college without fulfilling their goals. The reasons why are under intense scrutiny at the national, state, regional, and local levels.

Discussion about improving completion rates has been accompanied by laments over the lack of academic readiness of many incoming college students. While there are many reasons why students do not meet their academic goals in community colleges, policymakers, researchers, and practitioners have honed in on developmental education, or remediation, as a major culprit. One article went so far as to call it "Higher Ed's Bermuda Triangle" (Esch, 2009). New research shows the extent of the remediation problem descriptively, in terms of the numbers of students deemed unprepared for college-level courses, and has also questioned the effectiveness of the remedial courses in which a large proportion of entering community college students enroll. Still other studies have demonstrated that the assessments colleges use to sort students into remedial or college-level work may not be good measures of students' skills or aptitude. These studies are discussed in more detail below.

Thus, many educators, education leaders, and policymakers now view developmental education, as it has been traditionally organized and taught, as an obstacle to student success rather than as a support. Students have affirmed this perspective as well when discussing the years it can take to complete required developmental education sequences (Venezia, Bracco, & Nodine, 2010). In what is probably the strongest statement to this effect, Stan Jones (2013), the president of a nonprofit organization that works to increase college attainment, has said about remediation, "It's not possible to do worse than we're doing today." While there are no data to support this claim, such hyperbole is likely meant to stress a need for a new approach, and many are in agreement that fixing remediation will go a long way toward improving college completion rates. As a result, there is a great deal of experimentation underway across the nation. This experimentation is proceeding at different levels—state, institution, and classroom—and with varying amounts of evidence as a foundation.

Below, we briefly review the research evidence on both remedial assessment and the effectiveness of remedial coursework. We then describe an approach referred to as "acceleration" that is becoming a popular way to reform how and when remedial education is provided. Next, we provide some examples of how different acceleration models are being implemented in the field. We describe some instances in which acceleration strategies have been piloted, evaluated, and then expanded, and contrast this approach with examples where state legislators or system leaders have wrought complete overhauls of remediation without those steps. We conclude with cautions about mandated and rapid reform in advance of a strong evidence base.

Evidence on Remedial Assessment and Placement

Entering community college students are typically assessed using a computer-adaptive instrument (ACCUPLACER and COMPASS are commonly used) to determine readiness for college-level coursework or need for remediation (Hodara, Jaggars, & Karp, 2012; Hughes & Scott-Clayton, 2011; Venezia et al., 2010). The majority of students at community colleges are advised that they require some developmental coursework; many are told that they will need a sequence of two or more semester-long courses. More than half of all entering community college students do enroll in at least one remedial course, and others are assigned to do so but never enroll (Bailey, 2009; Bailey, Jeong, & Cho, 2010).

Recent studies that use rigorous methods to examine the effectiveness of remediation have found mixed or negative results of remedial courses on student progression (Bettinger & Long, 2005, 2009; Calcagno & Long, 2008; Martorell & McFarlin, 2009). An analysis of the remediation "pipeline"—the authors tracked students who were assigned to courses three levels below college level—found that even when students passed one level, they did not necessarily enroll in the next. Developmental students left the pipeline all along the way, with the result that, for the particular sample studied, only 20% of the students originally referred to math remediation completed a college-level course within three years (Bailey et al., 2010). In addition, a study completed for Virginia's Community College system found that students who did not abide by their recommended placement in developmental education had similar rates of taking and passing the first college-level English or math course as students who did take a developmental course in the subject (Roksa, Jenkins, Jaggars, Zeidenberg, & Cho, 2009). Particularly with respect to English, there were no notable differences in passing rates between those students who were referred to developmental courses and took them, and those referred who did not.

In light of this new evidence, and additional studies showing that student performance on the above-mentioned placement tests are weakly correlated with success in college-level courses (Belfield & Crosta, 2012; Scott-Clayton, 2012), instructors, institutions, and states are implementing new practices and policies designed to assess and address students' academic gaps in a more fine-grained and prompt manner. These changes respond to the criticism of the status quo in assessment, placement, and remedial curricula, as well as to pressure from the College Completion Agenda to help students move more quickly toward earning degrees and other credentials.

This chapter provides examples of massive reform efforts underway, starting with institutionally and classroom-based changes focused on accelerating developmental education. Acceleration is one of the most common approaches to reforming remediation and entails changes to the content and pacing of developmental instruction so that students can fill in their academic holes more quickly. Acceleration can take many forms and is discussed below.

An Example of Institutional- and Classroom-Based Reform: Accelerating Developmental Education

Acceleration in developmental education is a strategy used by community colleges to reduce the amount of time students spend in remediation and allow them to enroll more quickly—or immediately—in courses leading to certificates or degrees. Acceleration requires rethinking the content to be taught, in addition to the time frame in which the learning occurs. In a traditional series of developmental education courses, there are multiple "loss points" at which students tend to drop out. As discussed above, while many students pass one or more courses in a developmental series, most never progress to the point at which they take college-level course work.

Acceleration models seek to reduce the number of loss points as well as minimize the time required for students to get college ready, so that more students earn a certificate or degree and in a shorter period of time (Edgecombe, 2011; Hern & Snell, 2010). From a review of the literature and of current practices, Nodine, Dadgar, Venezia, and Bracco (2013) discuss a number of key principles of current acceleration programs that appear to be supporting greater rates of success than traditional developmental education models. First, they help students avoid developmental education whenever possible (e.g., by weighting high school grade point average more heavily in the placement process). Second, these models also revise the developmental education curriculum to shorten the sequence, align it with transfer-level and career technical coursework, and make it more rigorous. Third, the models provide additional student supports that are integrated with coursework. They may provide remediation simultaneously with courses that lead to credentials, and/or customize and contextualize remediation along multiple academic and career pathways so that students learn math or language arts concepts based on their specific needs and on their desired instructional programs. Finally, these models monitor progress at regular intervals based on demonstrated competency rather than on seat time.

In seeking to accelerate student learning in developmental education, colleges are drawing from a combination of models, based on local contexts, subject matter, and student needs. Some approaches include simultaneous enrollment in courses leading to a credential (mainstreaming), compression and sequence redesign, and modularization. With simultaneous enrollment, students bypass one (or more) courses in a developmental education series and enroll in either transfer-level courses with additional support or courses leading to stackable certificates that may not require remediation immediately. Students who enroll directly in transfer-level courses receive additional supports, such as an additional academic support course or intensive tutorials. This approach requires effective career and educational planning so that students understand how their program coursework prepares them for various career options.

When courses are compressed or the course sequences are redesigned, it opens up opportunity to rethink the curriculum to reduce redundancies. This is often done by aligning with the requirements of specific fields of employment, and/or with what instructors believe is essential for students to learn. This can include significantly changing course content, combining courses in existing sequences, pairing courses, and providing students with additional support.

For the third model, modularization, traditional semester-long developmental courses are divided into discrete learning units, or modules, that are designed to improve a specific competency or skill. Students are required to pass customized interventions consisting of only the modules they need and no more. Modularization requires very fine-grained and effective diagnostic assessments in order to identify the specific learning needs for each student. While this tailored approach holds promise, modularization may make the curriculum too disjointed and insufficiently contextualized for some students, and self-paced modules may not be appropriate for others who do not have good time-management skills.

Accelerated Learning Program of the Community College of Baltimore County

While many efforts to accelerate developmental education courses are contained to individual courses, the Community College of Baltimore County's (CCBC) Accelerated Learning Program (ALP) is an instructive example of an accelerated developmental education strategy that was successfully scaled up within one institution. CCBC piloted the new format, participated in a rigorous third-part evaluation of it, and based on positive results scaled it to include almost all eligible students.

The creation of the Accelerated Learning Program at the Community College of Baltimore County was prompted by data from the college that showed the majority of students beginning in developmental education were not persisting through the developmental sequence to the college-level course. As described above, the sequence presented too many exit opportunities, and students who passed one course did not necessarily register for the next. Thus, administrators and faculty saw a need for change.

The model that was developed was mainstreaming or "coenrollment"—students who normally would be placed in the first level of developmental writing (English 052) before being allowed to enroll in English 101 would instead be enrolled simultaneously in the two courses. English 101 would contain a mix of college-ready and almost-college-ready students, and the companion English 052 was redesigned as a supportive, workshop-style course to reinforce the English 101 curriculum. And, in addition to addressing students' writing challenges, the course would try to assist with barriers to students' college success generally.

ALP was piloted in 2007 with 10 sections. Importantly, many students at the college were still enrolled in the traditional developmental writing course, so an external evaluator could compare outcomes of students in the new versus the old format. The results were positive in that ALP students completed college-level English at higher rates and also had higher rates of persistence to the next academic year (Cho, Kopko, Jenkins, & Jaggars, 2012; McKusick, Adams, Ashby, & Cho, 2013). Encouraged by these findings, CCBC gradually increased the number of sections of ALP so that in the fall of 2012, ALP was serving 1,064 students in 133 sections. CCBC administrators and faculty are currently assisting other colleges in implementing similar coenrollment models. While ALP is an example of a college-based scaling effort, state systems and, in unprecedented moves, state legislatures are now beginning to mandate changes in the provision of developmental education.

State-Based Examples of Developmental Education Reform

While individual institutions and instructors are experimenting with ways to reform developmental education, states are now jumping into the fray with large-scale changes. Below, we provide some specific examples, contrasting these approaches and noting any evidence supporting them.

California's Basic Skills Initiative.   In 2006, the California Community Colleges' Chancellor's Office started the Basic Skills Initiative (BSI)—a grant-funded initiative focused on improving developmental education, or basic skills, that was part of the strategic planning process. The BSI essentially provided funds for local experimentation and included two main strands: (a) allocating supplemental funding for colleges to address basic skills needs and (b) providing grants for professional development, focused on faculty and staff in basic skills and in English as a Second Language instruction. A distinct feature of the BSI was training statewide for adjunct and noncredit faculty, since they teach the majority of developmental education courses, and approximately half of the students in developmental education and English as a Second Language enroll in noncredit programs and courses. The BSI led to several publications focused on helping the field at large, including a literature review (available at http://www.cccbsi.org/publications) and a self-assessment tool that helps colleges identify their strengths and weaknesses with regard to developmental education (available at http://www.cccbsi.org/self-assessment).

The 2011 Basic Skills Leadership Institute focused on launching acceleration pilots with 14 colleges. In that year, over 80 colleges across the state had taken part in The California Acceleration Project, an effort to support instructional shifts in English and math in California's community colleges. Within that network, instructors shortened developmental sequences, reduced the number of "loss points" for students, and focused on the "most essential skills and ways of thinking required in a good college-level course" (http://3csn.org/developmental-sequences).

Wholesale Developmental Education Reform in Virginia and North Carolina.   In contrast to incentivizing local experimentation, such as was done through the BSI, or approaches to reform that pilot new models and scale up the most promising or most effective, some states are in the process of entirely overhauling the content and delivery of remedial education. The community college system offices of both Virginia and North Carolina have embarked upon comprehensive change to developmental assessment, placement, and coursework (see Asera, 2011; Hodara et al., 2012). State task forces and committees were convened to determine the principles for developmental redesign, and in both states acceleration became a primary strategy. The final approaches were quite similar: modularization of developmental math content, so that students could take only the content needed, and integration of developmental reading and writing into one developmental English program. A modularized curriculum requires a more fine-grained approach to assessment, so new instruments have been developed for placement.

Elimination of Traditional Remediation in Connecticut.   Concerned about the lack of academic progress of developmental students, the Connecticut state legislature and Governor Malloy signed "An Act Concerning College Readiness and Completion" in August 2012. The Act directs the ways in which Connecticut State Colleges and Universities may provide remedial support. Beginning in fall 2014, remediation must be embedded within entry-level courses for students who, based on multiple assessments, are deemed unlikely to succeed without such support or may be provided via a one-semester intensive college readiness program. The Act was developed in reaction to existing practice in which students who are the least prepared complete three semesters of remedial work.

Reforming Assessment and Placement in Florida.   Recent Florida legislation will transform developmental assessment, placement, and delivery in that state. Florida Senate Bill 1720, signed by the governor in May 2013, strikes out previous policy prohibiting students from enrolling in college-level courses until they show readiness via the common placement test. Instead, the new policy allows students with a Florida high school diploma to choose themselves whether to take the test or enroll in remedial coursework. In addition, all state system institutions must deliver developmental education in an accelerated, modularized, contextualized, corequisite or compressed format, and annually report student success data related to each strategy.

Discussion

The landscape of developmental education has changed dramatically in a very short time. Remediation has gone from being a fairly obscure and understudied facet of community college instruction to an object of great scrutiny, classroom-level experimentation, and statewide legislation. At the heart are concerns that, for students who go directly from high school to college, a great deal of time and money is being spent on, and by, students who should arrive already college ready. Those concerns, combined with scarce resources and a consequent focus on efficiency and effective use of public dollars, have called traditional developmental education practices into question.

We are seeing reform catalyzed in different ways, through institutional experimentation, state-provided funding for cross-institutional knowledge-sharing and professional learning, state-led consensus-driven comprehensive change, and legislated mandate. This experimentation is proceeding more quickly than the field's ability to understand what is effective, for whom, and how. It is not clear that there is sufficient evidence to support legislative mandates reducing the amount of developmental instruction permitted or allowing students to decide their developmental needs for themselves.

Only a few years ago, in a review of the literature on developmental assessment and placement, researchers wrote that, "the current national trend appears to be toward state standardization of assessment and enforcement of mandatory placement, suggesting that practitioners and state policymakers believe assessment contributes to students' success" (Hughes & Scott-Clayton, 2011, p. 4). The "right to fail" philosophy that held sway in the 1970s, spurning mandatory testing, placement, and course prerequisites in support of college students making their own educational decisions, appeared to have been rejected. Now, while states such as Virginia and North Carolina follow the centralized and standardized approach, the new Florida legislation provides student leeway. The popularity of the acceleration strategy, motivated by students' poor persistence through traditional developmental education course sequences and bolstered by early evidence from programs such as ALP, exemplifies another shift: a greater focus on what is happening inside classrooms. This is a fundamental change for higher education, where classroom practice is often not part of the reform conversation, unlike in the K–12 arena.

These developments underscore the importance of the role of research in any effort for broad change. In the case of remedial education, research showed that current practices were not having the desired effect, and this new knowledge, combined with a new national focus on student success, led to urgency for change. At the same time, research on some effective practices was just beginning to emerge. As broad-scale change proceeds in a few states, it is critical that we measure the effects of these reforms on student outcomes, so that evidence drives the way forward.

References

Asera, R. (2011). *Innovation at scale: How Virginia community colleges are collaborating to improve developmental education and increase student success.* Boston, MA: Jobs for the Future.

Bailey, T. (2009). Challenge and opportunity: Rethinking the role and function of developmental education in community college. In A. C. Bueschel & A. Venezia (Eds.), *New Directions for Community Colleges: No. 145. Policies and practices to improve student preparation and success* (pp. 11–30). San Francisco, CA: Jossey-Bass.

Bailey, T., Jeong, D. W., & Cho, W. S. (2010). Referral, enrollment, and completion in developmental education sequences in community colleges. *Economics of Education Review, 29*(2), 255–270.

Belfield, C. R., & Crosta, P. M. (2012). *Predicting success in college: The importance of placement tests and high school transcripts* (CCRC Working Paper No. 42). New York, NY: Columbia University, Teachers College, Community College Research Center.

Bettinger, E. P., & Long, B. T. (2005). Remediation at the community college: Student participation and outcomes. In C. A. Kozeracki (Ed.), *New Directions for Community Colleges: No. 129. Responding to the challenges of developmental education* (pp. 17–26). San Francisco, CA: Jossey-Bass.

Bettinger, E. P., & Long, B. T. (2009). Addressing the needs of underprepared students in higher education: Does college remediation work? *Journal of Human Resources, 44*(3), 736–771.

Calcagno, J. C., & Long, B. T. (2008). *The impact of postsecondary remediation using a regression discontinuity approach: Addressing endogenous sorting and noncompliance* (NBER Working Paper No. 14194). Cambridge, MA: National Bureau of Economic Research.

Cho, S.-W., Kopko, E., Jenkins, D., & Jaggars, S. S. (2012). *New evidence of success for community college remedial English students: Tracking the outcomes of students in the accelerated learning program (ALP)*. New York, NY: Community College Research Center, Teachers College, Columbia University.

Edgecombe, N. (2011). *Accelerating the academic achievement of students referred to developmental education* (CCRC Working Paper No. 55). New York, NY: Community College Research Center, Teachers College, Columbia University.

Esch, C. (2009). Higher ed's Bermuda Triangle. College Guide Blog in *Washington Monthly*. Retrieved from http://www.washingtonmonthly.com/college_guide/feature/higher_eds_bermuda_triangle.php?page=all

Hern, K., & Snell, M. (2010). *Exponential attrition and the promise of acceleration in developmental English and math*. Hayward, CA: Chabot College.

Hodara, M., Jaggars, S. S., & Karp, M. M. (2012). *Improving developmental education assessment and placement: Lessons from community colleges across the country* (CCRC Working Paper No. 51). New York, NY: Community College Research Center, Teachers College, Columbia University.

Hughes, K. L., & Scott-Clayton, J. (2011). *Assessing developmental assessment in community colleges* (CCRC Working Paper No. 19). New York, NY: Community College Research Center, Teachers College, Columbia University.

Jones, S. (2013, July). *Transforming remedial education to improve postsecondary attainment*. Presented at the American Youth Policy Forum, Washington, DC.

Martorell, P., & McFarlin, I. J. (2009). *Help or hindrance? The effects of college remediation on academic and labor market outcomes*. Santa Monica, CA: RAND and University of Michigan.

McKusick, D., Adams, P., Ashby, J., & Cho, S.-W. (2013). *Lessons learned from five years of developmental education acceleration*. Retrieved from http://ccrc.tc.columbia.edu/presentation/lessons-learned-from-five-years-of-developmental-education-acceleration.html

Nodine, T., Dadgar, M., Venezia, A., & Bracco, K. (2013). *Acceleration in developmental education*. San Francisco, CA: WestEd.

Roksa, J., Jenkins, D., Jaggars, S. S., Zeidenberg, M., & Cho, S.-W. (2009). *Strategies for promoting gatekeeper course success among students needing remediation: Research report for the Virginia community college system*. New York, NY: Columbia University, Teachers College, Community College Research Center.

Scott-Clayton, J. (2012). *Do high-stakes placement exams predict college success?* (CCRC Working Paper No. 41). New York, NY: Columbia University, Teachers College, Community College Research Center.

Venezia, A., Bracco, K. R., & Nodine, T. (2010). *One-shot deal? Students' perceptions of assessment and course placement in California's community colleges*. San Francisco, CA: WestEd.

ANDREA VENEZIA *is an associate professor of Public Policy and Administration at the California State University, Sacramento, and the associate director of the University's Institute for Higher Education Leadership & Policy (IHELP).*

KATHERINE L. HUGHES *is the executive director of Community College and Higher Education Initiatives at the College Board.*

5

Content standards have been identified in America as a solution to the declining rate of student success in the public education system. But content standards are not a "silver bullet," for a number of reasons. This chapter presents an intersegmental approach to vertical curriculum alignment that returns questions of student readiness to the shared experience of educators and students.

Working Across the Segments: High Schools and the College Completion Agenda

Shelly Valdez, David Marshall

Community colleges have for years admitted waves of students brought up in standards-oriented classrooms. Simultaneously, colleges have wrestled with their own internal struggles around increasing rates of remediation, an issue that attempts to reduce the risk of underprepared students from leaving before completion of their degrees. State standards are not new, but in recent years, with the development and advent of the Common Core State Standards (CCSS), many states have renewed their efforts to increase student success with a set of common, rigorous standards shared across states. Even those few states that have rejected the Common Core have revised or reinvigorated their own educational standards in light of recent trends in education. A single premise underlies these efforts: designating what students should know and be able to do at the completion of each grade level or course equips educators to set targets by which students climb a ladder of ever-increasing demand and proficiency toward college and career readiness. The focus on an articulated pathway toward higher education makes standards like the Common Core a key component of the completion agenda, which assumes that by developing in learners the knowledge and skills expected of them as they enter college (the focus of our discussion), success in college and career will increase. But given those waves of standards-educated students and college struggles with remediation, the success of these new efforts seems uncertain.

NEW DIRECTIONS FOR COMMUNITY COLLEGES, no. 164, Winter 2013 © 2014 Wiley Periodicals, Inc.
Published online in Wiley Online Library (wileyonlinelibrary.com) • DOI: 10.1002/cc.20080

For any standards-based strategy to contribute productively to increased numbers of students ready for college the standards must be aligned with college-level expectations. In the development of the Common Core, for example, drafters consulted assessment data relating to college- and career-ready performance and vetted the documents with a group of college and university faculty. According to a report by the bipartisan education reform group Achieve (2012), "The claim that the CCSS define both the core academic knowledge and skills students need for success in college and careers is accurate" (p. 15). In Texas, a gap-analysis suggests the state's college readiness standards cover additional areas of college readiness that are missing from the national standards (Texas Higher Education Coordinating Board, 2010). In each, an optimistic sense of alignment, if perhaps incomplete according to some, permeates the statement.

The Achieve (2012) report goes on, however, to note, "Of course, the CCSS only identify those skills—it is up to teachers and their use of pedagogy and instruction to help students master the content and skills called for in the CCSS" (p. 15). That same observation could be made of the Texas standards and applies to any such standards documents. Therein lies the problem. According to the College Board (2010), the standards themselves are only one component of the solution to the college-readiness issues they seek to remedy:

> Content standards outline the knowledge and skills students should attain at each level of their education across different subjects. These standards serve as the foundation for every other component of raising student achievement. Although each state has the structure in place to articulate the content standards their students should meet, various problems exist across the current state frameworks, including a lack of common assessment measures, different definitions of progress, problems associated with students transferring across state lines and different expectations for teacher training. Such problems ultimately hinder student preparation for college and career. High-quality and rigorous content standards are by no means the silver bullet for raising student achievement, but they are essential for all other strategies to be integrated into a coherent effort toward higher achievement. (p. 9)

Content standards have been identified in America as a solution to the declining rate of student success in the public education system. But as the College Board's statement indicates, content standards cannot be a "silver bullet," since they are accompanied by a variety of hurdles to the development of an education system that better facilitates that success. The persistence of remediation in community colleges, despite the emphasis on standards in K–12 education, confirms as much. As we will argue, one way through these hurdles is a particular intersegmental approach to vertical curricular alignment that brings together K–12 and postsecondary faculty to tackle some of the standards issues from "both sides" so that students

NEW DIRECTIONS FOR COMMUNITY COLLEGES • DOI: 10.1002/cc

can more smoothly transition from one segment to the next. For colleges the benefit, we will argue, is a reduction in remediation and an increase in student success, translated here as completion.

Colleges and the Common Core

With the CCSS in various stages of implementation across the United States, there has been increased understanding of the need to involve postsecondary education in the discussion. This is a positive turn, in our view, for a number of reasons. Educators from both secondary and postsecondary education have a stake in the successful implementation of CCSS and their alignment to postsecondary education. After all, the preparedness of students exiting high schools and entering colleges impacts student success, and therefore completion, in college. As the nation addresses increasing completion, the preparation of students to be successful in postsecondary education is paramount.

As we have already said, despite the standards movement at the state level, remediation of students entering college has not decreased in the last decade. History has shown that aligning high school curricula to standards does not ensure high school exit skills are aligned to college entrance expectations, and there are implications at the postsecondary level for remedial or developmental education that arise from CCSS implementation. The cost of unprepared students in postsecondary is a fiscal drain on families, education institutions, and states, as well as an emotional drain on students who believed they were prepared for college. Unfortunately, a high school diploma does not necessarily mean a student is college ready—a fact that colleges rehearse each year with new cohorts of incoming students.

A primary goal of the CCSS is to bring students to college- and career-ready status. So it stands to reason that postsecondary institutions, which are receiving these students, must be involved in the discussion of the alignment of exit skills and entrance expectations. For that reason, our discussion below does not isolate the relationships between secondary schools and community colleges, despite the focus of this volume. Bringing together faculty from different educational systems, K–12, community colleges, and four-year universities, not only improves communication and networking among educators but also ensures that courses articulate with a smooth transition between segments. That principle holds true not just for the transition from secondary to community colleges but also for the transition between community colleges and the universities to which their students often transfer. Doing this work without all segments involved is like trying to climb a ladder without all the rungs. When one segment is excluded, not only is its input missing, but so is their buy-in to the process and its results. For true educational change to take place, all segments' faculty voices must be well represented and heard. The inclusive nature of the model we will describe benefits community colleges disproportionately, though, since they stand to receive better prepared students, see their own students complete degrees with greater frequency, *and* achieve greater success in transfer institutions for those students transitioning to four-year institutions.

Yet, there is wide variation among states in the extent to which postsecondary education is involved in the CCSS discussion. Furthermore, there are issues of both process and content: whom to involve and when; how to capitalize on the expertise of all segments; and what steps are best taken and in what order, when analyzing and aligning CCSS and curricula across segments.

The approach we will describe is one driven by collaboration among educators within regions to align curricula by explicating what content standards mean within the unique educational contexts of those regions and their coming to consensus about both the entrance and exit competencies expected between the education segments: K–12 and higher education. Among the benefits of this approach are reduced remediation and increased student success, retention, and completion. Moreover, this approach returns questions of student readiness to the shared experience of educators and students by emphasizing meaningful authentic assessment.

A Structure for the Process

There are obviously a number of methods that would work to get to alignment. What is necessary is a process that delineates and aligns entrance and exit expectations while maintaining curricular integrity and academic freedom within and across institutions. In addition (as elaborated upon below), it is necessary that such a process deeply involves faculty and allows for collaboration of faculty across institutions, regions, and even across educational segments (e.g., high school, college, and university faculty working together to come to consensus about the content and rigor of the aligned expectations). We will describe a process in which faculty from high schools, colleges, and universities collaborated on developing a means of aligning curricula, a process with demonstrated success. The project from which we have abstracted this model originates from work done under the guidance of the California Partnership for Achieving Student Success (Cal-PASS), in its years operated from the San Diego area's Grossmont-Cuyamaca Community College District. Under the banner of Cal-PASS, Dr. Valdez helped to facilitate the work on which we have based this model, heretofore unpublished, and Dr. Marshall has worked to replicate it in another region of Southern California with faculty from each of the educational segments. The importance of the faculty-led nature of the project cannot be overstated.

It is faculty who, by training and through their daily interactions with their students, are the experts in both discipline content and pedagogy, and it is they who must be the leaders in unpacking the standards and expectations for those students. It is faculty who will implement the content of the unpacked and aligned standards and who, therefore, must understand their meanings and nuances in order to fully put them to practice in their classrooms.

Prior to any process of this sort, however, it must be clear that the work cannot be accomplished unless there is an environment of safety within which those faculty can discuss, argue, resolve, and reach consensus as equal colleagues regardless of their position along the educational spectrum (K–12, college, university, and beyond) or their institution. The success of this work depends on faculty participants understanding that they teach the same students at different points in time and that each faculty member works with the success of all their students in mind. Faculty participants each bring a unique perspective to the table and must feel free to participate and contribute as equal colleagues. Hierarchies allow for important voices to be silenced, so titles, degrees, and other emblems of status are left outside the door. Inside the meeting room, the group consists of equal colleagues with equal voices working for the betterment of all their students in their region.

Because all voices are considered equal, decisions are made by the full group. Group members feel free to voice minority opinions and those opinions receive full consideration by the group. Having established trust, safety, and quality among its members, the most successful groups continue their discussions until decisions are reached by consensus with all perspectives taken into consideration.

Intersegmental collaborations must be thoughtfully planned, intentionally established, and rigorously implemented. Without the investment of time and attention to process and content of the discussions, the products of this work are likely to be inadequate, inconsistent, and difficult, if not impossible, to implement. Any change to systems, methods, or culture needs and deserves to be supported by finding time and resources for the necessary professional development to implement that change. Certainly participation in the intersegmental alignment is a form of professional development and works to keep segments connected and consistent over time. But for the entire system to adopt a change, all faculty members must be made aware of, and trained in, these efforts.

For any educational change implementation to take hold, become part of the culture of the institutions involved, and sustain itself, faculty and administrators must be aware of and accepting of support by the leadership of all districts, institutions, local, regional, and state leaders. Lack of support from any of these levels can stop funding or time devoted to the efforts, either of which likely will have detrimental effects on any change effort.

Regularly scheduled meetings are imperative for many reasons. Participants need the time on an ongoing basis to build a trusting and collaborative workspace and need to be able to count on their work continuing and building on itself over a period of time to completion. Irregular, infrequent meetings lead participants to believe that their work is not important enough to be supported on a regular basis. Nor does it allow them the time to build relationships and trust necessary for intersegmental work to move from finger points to handshakes. In addition, irregular participation by members means that work is delayed by having to initiate and orient new participants into the work.

Three Stages to Alignment

Our model for curriculum alignment involves three stages: (a) development of outcomes, (b) gap analysis, and (c) development of illustrative assignments. Each stage has several steps and the steps are iterative throughout the stages.

Stage one of the alignment process brings faculty together, with resources such as their syllabi, student learning outcomes (SLOs), and course outlines with reference to existing standards, to brainstorm exit and entrance outcomes of the courses or content to be aligned. Outcomes are written in SMART form (specific, measurable, appropriate, relevant, and time bound), with this form constantly being refined along the stages and steps of the process.

This part of the process always results in lively discussions and debates as faculty unpack their own interpretations of standards and SLOs. It is often the case that faculty find themselves surprised at either the types of concepts that are taught by others or the breadth and depth with which a concept is taught by another faculty member school, institution, or educational segment. For example, after participating in this stage, many English faculty have been surprised to find that at the high school level, prior to Common Core State Standards, English courses focused on literature. At the community college level, they often focused on grammar and syntax, and at the university level on expository reading and writing skills. In math groups, participating in the alignment process, high school teachers are often taken aback by the fact that concepts they teach in depth are not used or covered in any depth by their higher education colleagues.

In addition, the vocabulary used by faculty is not standardized or consistent across institutions and certainly not from high schools to college. In fact, sometimes vocabulary is used inconsistently across faculty members within a single department. At one alignment meeting, faculty were asked what they wanted their students to do when they asked them to analyze a reading or readings. Some said, it meant to break down the reading into parts, others said they wanted students to compare and/or contrast, while still others wanted their students to describe. It is no small wonder that alignment is not an easy process and that it has not been undertaken automatically and consistently in the past.

Once brainstormed lists are developed, duplicates are removed and consensus arrived with respect to which are imperatives and which are optional, depending on the institution or faculty member.

Stage two begins with the lists of entrance and exit expectations upon which a gap analysis is performed to check for missing or superfluous outcomes. Some missing expectations are found in earlier courses and are so noted. Others are gaps in the curriculum or course sequence that need to be added and accounted for. During this process, each outcome is mapped to the SLO or standard it represents.

Stage three takes the now-aligned entrance and exit expectations and develops sample or illustrative assignments that exemplify the intended level of rigor. Contextualized assignments are encouraged. These are then field tested by faculty in their own classrooms and, as sometimes occurs, assignments or expectation outcomes are revised as necessary. Finally, the outcomes are refined a final time to ensure they follow the SMART parameters.

The result of these stages is a set of exit expectations that are in line with the entrance expectations of the subsequent courses with examples of assignments to ensure as much as possible both vertical and horizontal consistency for students regardless of institution.

Armed with the work of the previous steps, districts and institutions can be assured that their students are prepared deeply and broadly, and at consistent levels of rigor to meet the demands of increasingly complex subject matter and skill levels. Community colleges, in other words, can enroll students with confidence in their levels of learning, because community college faculty have collaborated in building the structures that prepared those students for the college classroom. That is the model in an abstract form. To demonstrate the process, we will describe the pilot project that generated the model and use that example to illustrate the benefits that result from it.

An Example of Successful Regional Alignment

A team of high school, community college, and university English instructors in a Southern California suburban community were concerned about curricular misalignment: a large proportion of their high school graduates were not prepared for college-level English courses. An unacceptably large proportion of their students were placed into remedial, noncollege credit courses upon matriculation. Based on evaluations of course pathway and performance data, the team focused their efforts on English Composition, the entry-level college course on expository (nonfiction) reading and writing. After identifying the reading and writing skills college students need to succeed in English Composition, the team designed an intervention, the English Curriculum Alignment Project (ECAP), which focused on improving these skills in the 9th through 12th grades. Then, faculty from the community college and university worked collaboratively with the English department of a local high school, helping them to infuse the identified skills into the high school's standards-based curriculum.

NEW DIRECTIONS FOR COMMUNITY COLLEGES • DOI: 10.1002/cc

Three quarters of the high school teachers using ECAP reported that they used more expository text than they had prior to their involvement in ECAP, and more than half said the project helped them cover more of California's state standards. Even more important: *enrollment in college-level courses increased.* In the six years after ECAP was introduced, high school student enrollment in college-level English courses grew from 36% to 57%, and enrollment in basic skills (also known as remedial or developmental) courses decreased. Student course success rates also increased. In 2005–2006, 44% of students taking English Composition at the local community college earned a C or better. Two years later, after implementation of ECAP, that figure rose 14 percentage points, to 58%.

After the success of the high school's students at their local community college, the college began admitting ECAP graduates into college-level composition courses regardless of their college placement scores. Eighty-two percent of the first group of ECAP students passed their English Composition courses at the community college compared to 68% of the general community college student population. Those who persisted to the next level course of English Composition were 100% successful. In the second year of ECAP, 86% were successful in their initial English Composition course and indications are that there will be continued success at the next level. The high school district then began the process of expanding ECAP to all of its high schools, with teachers from the program's early phase serving as mentors to the newest participants.

Alignment and College Completion

The success produced by ECAP is derived from a collaborative approach to education that emphasized faculty analysis and discussion of the types of prerequisite learning necessary for students to succeed. While a degree of alignment might be embedded in and implied by standards documents, without guided collaboration, the variability of interpretation can result in curricular practices prone to misalignment. Standards do not work to align high school exit expectations with college entrance expectations. The intersegmental approach to curriculum alignment is exemplified by ECAP works because it allows faculty in K–12 and postsecondary education to build agreed-upon, and therefore shared, definitions of and expectations for student learning. That common ground means that students can move through a truly articulated curricular sequence, the kind of articulation that recent efforts to create college- and career-aligned standards aspire to create.

As the College Board noted, rigorous standards for student learning offer an important component of planning for student success, but those standards require supporting efforts to overcome a variety of hurdles. Giving intersegmental faculty the opportunity to work together, as we have described, ensures that standards achieve their desired potential. In the case of ECAP, for example, more than half of the high school teachers said the

NEW DIRECTIONS FOR COMMUNITY COLLEGES • DOI: 10.1002/cc

project helped them cover more of California's state standards. That sense of synergy between standards and collaboratively generated innovations points to the benefits of a multifaceted approach to curricular alignment, one that does not expect standards documents to achieve productive benefits in isolation.

For community colleges, the stakes associated with standards are every bit as high as in K–12 education. While K–12 continues to operate under expectations set forth in Race to the Top, recent rhetoric from politicians seeks to tie federal support for higher education to institutional performance, measured in completion, among other factors. By engaging in the meaningful, faculty-driven, collaborative approach we have described, community colleges predispose their incoming students toward success and completion of degree programs. As the country puts its eggs in the aligned-standards basket, we fear that without the proper investment of faculty expertise and collaboration, efforts like Texas' standards and the Common Core will yield disappointing results. Enabling faculty to collaborate for student success will better ensure that new standards succeed too, leading to improved alignment between high school and college, and ultimately, college completion.

References

Achieve. (2012). *Understanding the skills in the Common Core State Standards.* Washington, DC: Author.

College Board. (2010). *College completion agenda state policy guide.* New York, NY: Author.

Texas Higher Education Coordinating Board. (2010). *Texas College and Career Readiness Standards more comprehensive than national standards.* Austin, TX: Author.

SHELLY VALDEZ *is the director of Educational Collaboration for the Institute for Evidence-Based Change.*

DAVID MARSHALL *is an associate professor of English at California State University and the co-chair of the Coachella Valley English Professional Learning Council.*

6

The Obama administration and the Lumina Foundation have been the principal drivers focusing the nation on increasing the number of high-quality degrees and credentials. Tuning, a faculty-driven process for defining clear student learning outcomes—what a student should know, understand, and be able to do—is one of the ways to support this goal.

Tuning Toward Completion

Marcus Kolb, Michelle Kalina, Adina Chapman

The Obama administration and the Lumina Foundation have been the principal drivers focusing the nation on increasing the number of high-quality degrees and credentials. The College Completion Agenda has as its Big Goal to increase the percentage of Americans with high-quality two- or four-year college degrees and credentials from 39% of the population to 60% by 2025, an increase of 23 million graduates above current rates (Russell, 2011). To be counted under Lumina's definition of high-quality degrees or credentials (including certificates), there must be clear and transparent learning outcomes leading to further education and employment.

Community colleges fulfill an important role, as the nation will not see these increases without full participation by community colleges. Degrees and certificates achieved from the community colleges have been shown to be highly correlated with increased earning over a high school diploma alone and provide great value to citizens (Gillen, Selingo, & Zatynski, 2013).

We also know that most students come to the community colleges seeking to transfer to a four-year university (Hoover, 2010; Panfil, 2012). A study of students in 1989–1990 found that 71% of community college students planned to transfer to a baccalaureate-granting institution (Bradburn, Hurst, & Peng, 2001). Unfortunately, more often than not, students intending on transfer will not complete a degree or certificate before they transfer to the university. Furthermore, many of these well-intentioned students never receive a baccalaureate and exit from higher education without a tangible degree or credential (Radford, Berkner, Wheeless, & Shepherd, 2010). This is why so many states are now developing strategies to increase the number of students transferring to the university with a degree.

New Directions for Community Colleges, no. 164, Winter 2013 © 2014 Wiley Periodicals, Inc.
Published online in Wiley Online Library (wileyonlinelibrary.com) • DOI: 10.1002/cc.20081

Community colleges and four-year universities must work together to ensure transfers lead to completion, as transfer is a principal function of the community colleges, and many students graduating from four-year universities have community college credits on their transcript. Furthermore, degrees must be of high quality, as determined by the discipline and potential employers. It is of little value to the nation if increases are met but the quality of the degrees is diluted. What the United States lacks is a comprehensive approach to defining learning outcomes representative of specific disciplines across different degree levels.

Tuning USA

Introduced to the United States by the Lumina Foundation, Tuning has been one method for ensuring quality. Begun in Europe, Tuning was an outgrowth of the establishment of the European Union's need to harmonize degrees across countries and to link the political objectives of the Bologna Process to the higher education sector. Although there are similarities between European and American higher education, a major distinction is that community colleges in America offer associate degrees and also transfer many students to four-year colleges and universities.

Tuning is a faculty-driven process to articulate what a student knows and is able to do in a given discipline at the point of degree. Typically, faculty from four- and two-year colleges and universities within a state meet by discipline to work through the Tuning process. Both public and private institutions within a state/region are included in the Tuning process, though participation is voluntary. Faculty members meet in their respective discipline groups to generate competencies and outcomes for their respective degrees.

Tuning involves creating a framework that establishes clear learning expectations for students in each subject area and sets forth clear responsibilities for institutions to invite all stakeholders (faculty, students, recent graduates, and employers) to have input into the process. It is critically important, however, that all programs being tuned retain their academic autonomy.

The objective is to better establish the quality and relevance of degrees in various academic disciplines. Lumina Foundation, the initiator and current cofunder of Tuning USA, enumerates a number of benefits arising from the Tuning process. First, the roles of higher education institutions become aligned. Second, the process facilitates retention, especially among students from underserved groups, by creating clear expectations for, and pathways to, degree completion. Third, Tuning simplifies the process for students transferring credits between institutions. Fourth, Tuning increases higher education's responsiveness to changes in knowledge and its application. Tuning also emphasized lifelong learning and important, but often undervalued, transferable skills. Finally, Tuning ensures that the applied skills associated with coursework align with societal needs and workforce demands.

What makes Tuning unique is that it intentionally includes collaboration among faculty from different institutions and institutional types across a state, professional organization, and/or groups of states. It breaks down silos and brings faculty together to talk about their discipline across many lines.

Tuning does not attempt to standardize curricula. As has been noted already, Tuning is a faculty-driven process that identifies an explicit core of learning outcomes within shared, discipline-specific competency areas. To that end, Tuning produces clear standards by which student success is defined, but it does not standardize. The core outcomes are not an attempt to standardize curricula or to create some sort of statewide or national curriculum.

In short, Tuning does not focus on curricula. The faculty experts who comprise the work groups may discuss their individual curricula as a means of making shared competencies and outcomes explicit, but not as a means of establishing a common curriculum. Individual faculty participants are responsible for assuring that they are attentive to those competencies and outcomes in their own curricula.

For example, English departments will agree that sensitivity to metaphor and other types of figurative language are an important point of learning in the discipline. One department might attend to this competency by making it an area of emphasis in literature survey classes. Another department might choose to offer a class in literary analysis that spends time on the topic. The area of learning is common between the departments, but the means by which they enable students to develop conversancy with it are particular to each instance. Tuning does not endeavor to stipulate all the competencies and outcomes in a discipline. Tuning seeks to identify the core competencies and outcomes of the discipline. In other words, Tuning gives faculty experts a chance to make explicit what in practice is already shared among them. Individual departments are made unique by how they teach those common competencies or by what they hold as important in addition to those common competencies.

Thus, identifying competencies and their subsequent outcomes does not limit the faculty's ability to approach the material as they see fit within their own institutions and classrooms. It only establishes what students should know and be able to do at the point of graduation in the discipline.

Value to Community Colleges

Tuning places all participating postsecondary educational institutions on equal footing. Faculty from community colleges are partners in defining the discipline core competencies. In fact, they might be closer to the local employment situation and better understand the needs of this stakeholder group than their four-year partners.

Community colleges benefit from participation in many ways. As with all institutions, there is increased clarity for students leading to the potential benefits noted earlier. With increases in contingent (or adjunct) faculty at colleges throughout the United States, defining the core competencies and student learning outcomes can assist in ensuring courses and sections are aligned within a department. Finally, agreement on what a student should know, understand, and be able to do upon leaving sets the stage for artic-ulation agreements benefitting transfer students. In Texas, Tuning led to broad-based, multiple institution agreements.

Early Tuning Efforts

A Tuning pilot began in 2009 with projects in three states—Indiana, Utah, and Minnesota. These states had previously expressed interest to the Lu-mina Foundation in trying the Tuning process and demonstrated the ca-pacity to bring discipline-specific faculty teams together to engage in the work. Each state elected specific disciplines to tune—Indiana selected ele-mentary education, history, and chemistry; Utah chose history and physics; and Minnesota opted for graphic design and biology. In each state, for each discipline, a team of faculty from two- and four-year institutions, public and private, was invited to an orientation to kick-start their work. All teams were given an aggressive timeline of nine months to complete the pilot project.

An initial, two-day training, drawing upon the Tuning expertise de-veloped in Europe, was provided to faculty teams from each of the pilot states. The faculty then returned to their respective campuses to start the work of meeting and determining student learning outcomes for associate, bachelor's, and master's degrees in their disciplines during the spring 2009 semester/quarter.

Using monthly electronic or face-to-face meetings, the teams followed the five-step Tuning process of suggesting outcomes, testing them with stakeholders, considering the stakeholder feedback, revising the outcomes, and considering the impact of their outcomes on their academic programs. The nine-month timeline proved too aggressive, and all of the teams re-quested extensions of the original grants in order to complete the work. Among the first lessons learned from the pilot was that this type of work takes time. Time to facilitate working relationships among faculty team members; time to identify and consult with stakeholders, including faculty, students, alumni, and employers; time to meet during challenging profes-sional schedules; and time to have the meaningful conversations required to distill the essence of a degree in a given field.

The pilot project also offered several additional lessons. Chief among these lessons was the challenge of how to collect feedback from stakehold-ers, particularly employers, in an effective and timely way. The international applications of Tuning suggested that surveying was a good method for collecting employer feedback, but the six different disciplines in the pilot had varying degrees of communication with employers, creating difficulty in knowing who to survey and how. For example, while identifying employers of elementary education graduates is relatively easy—they head to the school systems—identifying employers of history graduates was more challenging. Close examination of employers of history graduates showed a wide array of options, from museums to government positions to schools to publishing companies. While history faculty were delighted to learn of the diversity of destinations for their graduates, capturing the thoughts of these employers for adjusting the student learning outcomes was a challenge that stalled several of the Tuning teams. Instead of using the traditional survey route, several teams opted to convene focus groups of employers to test their outcomes. This practice became common among subsequent projects.

As the pilot projects began to conclude, we learned that faculty see value in collaborating with peers. Indeed, feedback often heard across the Tuning projects was the value of talking to discipline peers on other campuses and the opportunity for faculty to build trust about practice and intent.

A Statewide Tuning Effort

In Texas, faculty and state leaders saw Tuning as a vehicle to address a problem: the difficulty in transferring course credits among institutions. Most salient were issues related to engineering transfers. Most engineering students were seeing credit loss or the need to retake courses when leaving a community college and transferring to a four-year institution to complete their credential. Texas viewed Tuning as a way to create a transferrable engineering curriculum that would meet the student preparation needs of the four-year institutions and ensure that courses taken at the two-year level would transfer smoothly. This was the problem that energized faculty in Texas and gave their Tuning work a sense of purpose. In 2009, Texas convened four faculty teams in engineering—civil, industrial, electrical, and mechanical—and drew upon the expertise developed by the pilot states. Faculty teams met, tearing down their curriculum to its component learning outcomes and rebuilding it in a way that gave students the best opportunity to transfer their learning and credits in a productive fashion.

Texas was the first Tuning approach to actively seek to lay groundwork for the process by announcing the work at its inception to academic leadership and employers. These interactions created time and political space on campus for faculty to execute their work, and prepared employers for the surveys about student learning that were headed their way. Following on the success of the first four disciplines, Texas has continued to attack four new disciplines in each of the last three years. The work, led by the Texas Higher Education Coordinating Board, continues in earnest.

NEW DIRECTIONS FOR COMMUNITY COLLEGES • DOI: 10.1002/cc

In addition to the lesson of the value of meeting with key stakeholders prior to the faculty teams beginning their work, the Texas projects have also highlighted the need for champions, internal to the key institutions, in order to drive the work and ensure fidelity and success. Another lesson from Texas was the power of convening faculty across institutional lines. Faculty often regard the teaching of others with some level of suspicion—students learn and prosper in their own classes, but teaching at the other institution is of (perhaps) dubious quality. Tuning provides an opportunity to quickly break down these assumptions and suspicions. Once teams have been formed and discussions begin about the essence of a discipline, a transformation takes place. This transformation breaks down the typical suspicions and assumptions, leading to productive dialogue for the Tuning process and engendering trust for future collaborations. With students becoming increasingly mobile, the capacity to work across institutional lines to solve problems and improve teaching, learning, and assessment—to pick up the phone and call a colleague at another institution—is of great value.

Building Success With Facilitation

Kentucky was the first Tuning process facilitated by the Institute for Evidence-Based Change (IEBC). Four of the five disciplines selected had outside agencies dictating much of their curricula. The strategy used was to unpack the standards that were required of these disciplines by state agencies and national accreditors, and then work from unpacked standards back to their competencies and outcomes.

For example, the Nursing Tuning workgroup used the National League of Nursing (NLN) standards as their reference point to begin their alignment of Kentucky's Community and Technical College Systems' (KCTCS) associate's degree in nursing with the baccalaureate at Kentucky's four-year colleges and universities. Likewise, the business group referenced the standards of the Association to Advance Collegiate Schools of Business (AACSB) and the social work group tackled both the Council on Social Work Education (CSWE) as well as the Council for Standards in Human Service Education (CSHSE). Similarly, the elementary education workgroup unpacked their state education standards to facilitate alignment between the Associate in Applied Science degree in Education and teacher education programs at four-year colleges and universities. Grounding student learning outcomes—what a student knows, understands, and can do at different degree levels—in discipline standards went a long way toward ensuring degrees met the expectations of employers as well.

The Midwestern Higher Education Compact (MHEC) began tuning two new disciplines in fall 2011. It included the states of Indiana, Illinois, and Missouri and encompassed two disciplines—Marketing and Psychology. The MHEC project helps explore how Tuning is conducted in a regional context. This is the first time in the United States where Tuning has been implemented across state lines, regardless of type of institution (college or university) and regardless of where the institutions are situated (place), and represents a prototype for tuning disciplines on a national scale.

The MHEC group surfaced a critical unintended outcome of the Tuning work which is relevant to all disciplines. Working with the outputs of the Tuning effort, the Degree Specifications Document, faculty can map the competencies and outcomes back to the course or courses in their own curricula. The Degree Specifications Document and how it maps to courses are given to new faculty and contingent faculty to make clear what department expectations are, regardless of instructional method.

A National Discipline-Based Effort: The American Historical Association

The groundwork for a national Tuning project in history was laid when Tuning was first introduced in the United States in the states of Indiana, Minnesota, and Utah. That initial work Tuning history led to the American Historical Association's (AHA) interest in tuning history nationally. AHA took on the task of tuning the discipline on a national scale. They started the process with a group of six historians, representing the diversity of institutional types and the geographic diversity of the United States. This small group created a first draft of competencies and outcomes that were shared with a larger group of historians who represented various subdisciplines.

In June 2012, 62 historians were convened from across the country to review the initial work and begin the task of further unpacking and honing the competencies and outcomes. The historians met for a second weekend in February 2013 to review their progress and develop a method to obtain stakeholder feedback. They agreed on creating one survey for each of the identified stakeholder groups (faculty, alumni, current students, and employers), and that survey would be used across the United States.

Tuning and College Completion

As the Tuning work has evolved and matured in the United States, strategic thinking about its applications has also evolved. Where Tuning began as an exercise in improving and assuring academic quality, it was marketed as something of an antidote to the "completion agenda." Faculty are acutely aware that pressure is mounting to produce more graduates with academic credentials to both demonstrate the efficacy of institutional practice and to assure the growth and success of the economic future of the United States. However, faculty is naturally suspicious of any effort to produce more credentials. We can issue as many diplomas as we want, is often the cry, but who can be sure if the student has learned anything? Faculty feels great responsibility for assuring student learning, even if they are sometimes reluctant to submit to assessment. Tuning serves as a good counterpoint to the rising emphasis on completion.

Now that Tuning has been implemented in the United States for a few years, with many institutions and faculty, one thing has become increasingly clear. Tuning is not the antidote to the completion agenda. Rather, it has the potential to have a positive impact on increasing completion. Academic quality, clearly defined competencies, and thoroughly vetted student learning outcomes lead to more students completing degrees.

For first-generation college students or adults returning to higher education after years away, a chief concern is "what will I do and what will be expected of me while I am taking classes?" Tuning provides the opportunity to develop clear and accurate answers to those questions. A "tuned" curriculum makes sense to the uninitiated, with clear pathways through courses and a sense of outcomes, in terms of employment and next-level study options, for students who may not otherwise know what happens during and after a higher education.

As was demonstrated in Texas, Tuning is the ideal vehicle to resolve snags in the transfer process—another barrier to completion. With a well-aligned curriculum, where required learning is well understood and defined between transferring institutions, students will not lose time or credits. Loss of one or both is the enemy of completion, another barrier preventing students from achieving their academic goals.

As noted earlier, Tuning is not the only game in town in terms of addressing student learning outcomes. Efforts like the Liberal Education for America's Promise (LEAP) outcomes from AAC&U and the DQP are closely related to Tuning. All have similar aims—to discern the key components of student learning that should comprise a credential or degree and suggest how to assess those outcomes. In fact, another lesson learned in the Tuning work is that many attempts have been made in the past to define and propagate student learning outcomes, but Tuning remains distinct in that it provides a process to do the work, not a template of outcomes to be adopted.

Current higher education practice, which is sometimes absent well-articulated outcomes, can lack good measures of student performance. A higher education system that leads to more quality, and in turn, more completion, is built on the bedrock of regular, systematic assessment of student learning. There can be no better way to start than by defining the outcomes of the study of a discipline, as Tuning requires.

References

Bradburn, E. M., Hurst, D. G., & Peng, S. (2001). *Community college transfer rates to 4-year institutions using alternative definitions of transfer*. Washington, DC: National Center for Education Statistics.

Gillen, A., Selingo, J., & Zatynski, M. (2013). *Degrees of value: Evaluating the return on the college investment*. Washington, DC: Education Sector.

Hoover, E. (2010, April 27). *On transfer students and transfer friendliness.* Retrieved from http://chronicle.com/blogs/headcount/on-transfer-studentstransfer-friendliness/23499

Panfil, J. (2012, January 25). *Retaining college transfer students: Analyzing new data on a growing opportunity.* Retrieved from http://blog.noellevitz.com/2012/01/25/retaining-college-transfer-students-analyzing-data-growing-opportunity

Radford, A. W., Berkner, L., Wheeless, S. C., & Shepherd, B. (2010). *Persistence and attainment of 2003–04 beginning postsecondary students: After 6 years* (NCES 2011–151). Washington, DC: U.S. Department of Education, Institute of Education Sciences, National Center for Education Statistics.

Russell, A. (2011). *A guide to major U.S. college completion initiatives.* Washington, DC: American Association of State Colleges and Universities.

MARCUS KOLB is a project officer with the Lumina Foundation.

MICHELLE KALINA recently retired as the vice president for Tuning USA with the Institute for Evidence-Based Change.

ADINA CHAPMAN is director of Higher Education Policy Analysis at the College Board and former Tuning associate.

In California, public financial aid aimed at low-income students is not reaching some of the poorest students enrolled in community colleges. Outreach efforts to students are important, but high schools and community colleges must also make financial aid receipt a priority.

Unmet Need and Unclaimed Aid: Increasing Access to Financial Aid for Community College Students

Julia I. Lopez

This chapter discusses student outcomes and financial aid experience of more than one thousand very low income students who began their college journey in California's community colleges. I know about these students because they received scholarships funded by the College Access Foundation of California. I follow their progress closely, although I only know a few of them personally. Like a parent, I am invested in their success and committed to making college affordable by helping them secure all the financial aid available to them.

Every year, foundation grantees award more than 4,500 scholarships based on financial need, not merit, to California high school graduates. Approximately one in four of students who receive a scholarship enrolls in a community college. Students are expected to pursue an academic degree, so they are not representative of California's entire community college student population. Grantees report student level data to the foundation, including demographic characteristics, high school attended and graduation year, financial aid received, expected family contribution, and the name of the college in which the student initially enrolled. The foundation matches student information with the National Student Clearinghouse annually to document student persistence and graduation. The Institute for Higher Education Leadership and Policy (IHELP) at California State University Sacramento does an additional analysis of community college students. The Institute matches student records with the California Community College Chancellor's Office (CCCCO) statewide community colleges

New Directions for Community Colleges, no. 164, Winter 2013 © 2014 Wiley Periodicals, Inc.
Published online in Wiley Online Library (wileyonlinelibrary.com) • DOI: 10.1002/cc.20082

data system, which has information about students' credits attempted and earned, degrees or certificates earned, transfers, and financial aid received. This chapter is based on the IHELP's analysis of 1,355 students who graduated from high school between 2008 and 2011 and enrolled in community college within a year of graduation, supplemented by student information the foundation collects. To provide a human face to the numbers I met with three students who were kind enough to share their stories for this chapter. To protect their privacy I have changed their names.

Student Characteristics

According to the College Access Foundation of California's (2012) records most students are from very low income families and graduated from high schools that serve a large proportion of low-income students who qualify for free and reduced lunch. Seven of 10 students graduated from low-performing schools with a rank at or below the median of California's Academic Performance Index. Neither the state office of community college nor the foundation collects family income data so Pell eligibility is used as a proxy for low-income students. Over 90% were eligible for Pell Grants and six of 10 had no expected family contribution.

Because IHELP's (2013) report focuses on students who transition from high school to community college within a year of their high school graduation, most (97%) were under 19 years old when they enrolled in a college. Two thirds were young women and eight of 10 were first-generation college students. Almost three fourths (73%) were Latino students. Other students were Asian (10%), primarily from underrepresented groups like Vietnamese, Cambodian, Hmong; African American (9%); and White (6%), with the remainder (2%) unknown. Students' high school academic grade point averages (GPAs) ranged from below 2.0 to above 4.0. Nearly half (46%) of the students who enrolled in community college had GPAs below 3.0. Scholars are motivated and sufficiently articulate to compete successfully for scholarships, regardless of GPA.

There are many reasons students choose community college. The low cost of California community colleges is a big attraction. Maria graduated from high school with a 3.7 high school GPA. She lives with her mother and nieces. The household has a combined annual income of $12,000. "Money is scarce in my household and just recently I obtained an income of my own. This truly helps especially because my mom has responsibility of my two nieces while my older sister is in jail." The money she earns pays for her school and personal expenses. Since she was a little girl her dream was to become a doctor. She enrolled in the community college to save money for her education. Financial aid is helping make her dream come true. She received a Pell Grant, does not pay tuition fees because she received a California Community College Board of Governors (BOG) tuition fee waiver, and got a $1250 scholarship. Yet, the combined package only pays for two thirds of her cost of attendance; she pays the rest from her wages. Thanks to her high school GPA she also received a Cal Grant, the state's need-based grant; she has put it on hold until she transfers to a four-year college.

For others, like Carlos, community colleges offer a second chance. Carlos described himself as a "goof-off" in high school. He barely graduated, squeaking by with a 2.3 GPA. His father made it clear to him that if he wanted nice cars, a house, and money, he needed to buckle down and go to college. He is married, lives with his parents, and works for his dad to pay rent. He made it a point to secure all the financial aid available to him. A $5500 Pell Grant, a BOG tuition fee waiver, a $500 Federal Supplemental Educational Opportunity Grant (FSEOG), and a $1250 scholarship pay more than two thirds of his college cost of attendance. He is finishing his third year in the local community college, wants to be a nurse, and hopes to transfer to a four-year institution next fall.

Foundation scholarships are supposed to supplement other financial aid so grantees are expected to help students secure public financial aid. Maria and Carlos, who received public financial aid, are examples of students whose financial and enrollment situations the foundation envisioned. They are not the norm. In 2011–2012, less than half (47%) of all 18–24 year olds enrolled in California community colleges received a BOG waiver, only 26% received a Pell Grant, and 5% received a Cal Grant. A higher proportion of foundation students receive aid. More than three fourths (79%) secured BOG tuition fee waivers but only two thirds (67%) received Pell Grants. Even fewer, 33% received a Cal Grant. These students were fortunate to have help from our grantees; still we see that we are falling short for many of our eligible community college students. The largest proportion has their tuition fees waived, but fees account for less than 10% of the cost of attendance. For very low income students who only receive a BOG waiver the financial burden remains very high. Pell Grants, in addition to fee waivers, can make a considerable difference, reducing the students' financial burden to approximately one third the cost of attendance.

For a subset, private scholarships are the only source of available financial aid. Approximately 10% of our students are undocumented immigrants, also known as "dreamers," and were not eligible for public financial aid. Fortunately, California enacted its Dream Act in 2012 and, going forward, they will be eligible for Cal Grants and BOG waivers. The scholarship is the only assistance Anita received in 2012. She crossed the border as a young girl and has no papers. She lives with her parents and their combined family income is under $10,000. Extreme poverty and language did not deter her. She graduated from high school with a 3.5 GPA and enrolled in her local community college. "The fact that English was my second language did not discourage me from taking Honors and Advanced Placement English courses." Her dream is "to become a high school or college counselor so that I can make a difference in a student's education." Getting a college degree will also help her "provide for myself and my family, [including] my parents, as a way to thank them for all the sacrifices and struggles they have faced for my sake."

Only 4% of students ever took out loans. Maria, Carlos, and Anita said loans were scary to them. Many of their friends, they said, have large loans, which they got when they went to proprietary trade schools. They are also afraid of wasting the money on things besides school. Maria learned the importance of money management the hard way. When she received her first aid check, she spent most of it early on and ended the semester without enough money to cover her expenses. She now gives her grant check to her father who banks it for her and she has managed to save money for college. When asked, all three agreed that they would prefer to receive their financial aid in installments.

Foundation scholarships made a difference but not always in the ways I expected. These three students were all determined to go to college. Anita was already enrolled in the community college when she got her first scholarship. She and Carlos both used their first check to buy a car. They both explained that taking public transportation to the college took as long as three hours a day. Anita said this made taking evening classes impossible because bus schedules made the trip even longer.

Money is not the only reason all three chose to stay in the local community college: leaving home is a difficult step to take. Carlos, Maria, and Anita agreed that going to community college gave them a chance to get a better sense of what college would be like, "to get their feet wet." They were glad to have the opportunity to experience the ways in which college was different from high school. Though Maria and Anita were serious high school students, they both found the adjustment difficult and had to learn new study habits. Being at home and attending the local college was "a good way to start off."

Despite having a high GPA, including two years of algebra and geometry in high school, both Maria and Anita were assessed as needing remediation in math. The remedial math sections were full their first year, so they had to wait until their second year. When they enrolled in remedial math, they were frustrated. They were familiar with the material and they were not learning anything new. They will not be able to complete enough credits to transfer and know that remedial courses prolong their stay at the community college. Carlos, on the other hand, was always "good with the numbers" and needed remediation in English, which he successfully completed. But, despite his determination to finish, it has taken taking him three years.

This pattern of needing remediation regardless of high school record is common among our students. IHELP data show that, during the first year even students with the highest GPA have some remedial credits (2.2 credits), although half as many as students with lower GPAs (4.3 credits for those with GPAs between 3.5 and 3.0; and 5.5 credits for GPAs below 3.0). The majority of our students graduated from low-performing schools, which may explain this pattern. But, when I talk to students like Maria, Anita, and others who find themselves going over familiar material and not learning very much, I wonder if students really are not ready for college-level work or does the assessment process need to be revisited?

Does Financial Aid Make a Difference in Persistence and Completion?

We follow students by high school cohort. By 2012, four of 10 students (42%) of the class of 2008 transferred, completed a degree, or earned a certificate (College Access Foundation of California, 2012). Twenty percent of the class of 2009 and 5% of the class of 2010 had also done so. Academic preparation, using high school GPA as a proxy, appears to predict student outcomes in community colleges. Students who entered with a GPA under 3.0 are half as likely to transfer, get a degree, or a certificate as students with GPAs between 3.0 and 3.5; and one third as likely as students with the highest GPAs. The majority of students who transfer go to the California State Universities and one in five transfers to University of California campuses. IHELP also compared students who received financial aid to students who did not. Students who received BOG waivers and Pell Grants or Cal Grants completed more credits and earned a degree, certificate, or transferred at slightly higher rates (between 5 and 6 percentage points higher) than those who did not. The same difference held for students who are more recent graduates: those who received aid were more likely to be on track to transfer or complete a degree in two or three years than those that did not.

When the students are disaggregated by racial and ethnic groups differences and disparate outcomes become apparent. For example, Asian students are almost twice as likely to have completed a degree (26%), earned a certificate, or transferred as are Latino students (14%). Asians begin their community college career with higher GPAs than other groups: 70% of Asian students enrolling in community colleges have high school GPAs over 3.0 and half of them (36%) have GPAs over 3.5. While the proportion is not as high among Latinos, more than half of the Latino students (57%) who enroll in community colleges have GPAs over 3.0 and roughly half (26%) have GPAs above 3.5. There are differences in academic preparation; we don't think they fully explain the large difference in outcomes.

Asian students were the most likely to receive all forms of aid and Latino students were less likely to have done so. Only 73% of Latinos ever received a BOG waiver compared to 95% for Asians. Less than two thirds (64%) of Latinos received Pell Grants while 83% of Asians did so. Asians received the highest proportion of Cal Grants (59%) while only 30% of Latino students did so. These patterns are similar to national data (Santiago, 2012).

The differences in aid receipt may also explain the difference in attendance patterns. IHELP (2013) found that 90% of foundation scholars remain continuously enrolled in community colleges. While there is a slight difference in continued attendance between Latinos (90%) and Asians (95%), there is a larger difference in the proportion who, on average, attend full time. Asians have the higher percent of full-time attendance (91%), but only three fourths (75%) of Latinos do so. Not surprisingly, Asians accumulate more credits than Latinos, which in the end may explain the better transfer and degree rates. Financial aid is only one variable in the equation for successful student outcomes; but for very low income students, it could make a critical difference. The foundation partnered with the Bill and Melinda Gates Foundation to support performance-based scholarship demonstration using a random assignment. The results will be available in the fall of 2013. We will also continue to explore this further, as we gather more longitudinal data.

Do Institutional Practices Make a Difference?

Beginning in 2012, the foundation is expanding its efforts to increase FAFSA completion in high schools with large proportions of low-income students. Carlos, Anita, and Maria live in a region where the business community has made FAFSA completion a priority. The local school districts compete with each other and vie to see which high schools increased FAFSA completion the most. In the last two years, rates in three school districts increased 10 percentage points, from 47% to 57%. They hope to do even better next year.

Carlos thinks the message to students needs to change. He observed that too much emphasis is placed on how difficult FAFSA is to complete; he didn't find it that difficult. He believes the message should be more positive—there's money to go to college and this is how you do it. He compared the messages with those of military recruiters who came to his school. Recruiters emphasize the opportunity to get paid and secure a future education. Financial aid can pay for your education now, he said. From his perspective, schools should focus less on why college is important—all three understood that it is essential to get a high paying job—and more on the nuts and bolts of how to get the money.

The federal government initiative to simplify the FAFSA application process is very helpful. The federal government also initiated pilots to increase in selected school districts by making FAFSA application information available weekly so schools can monitor who has applied and has completed their application. This gives schools student information to reach out in a timely manner to those who have not applied or who have incomplete applications. The foundation is encouraging more high schools to make FAFSA completion a priority and an integral part of the high schools' services to students. Information on how each school did in 2012 and 2013 is available on the web (Education Trust-West, 2013). We are also urging the state's student aid commission to consider ways to make FAFSA and Cal Grant application data available in real time and more user friendly so that schools can intervene with individual students when FAFSA season begins for the 2014 academic year.

If students complete their FAFSAs in high school, does it guarantee they will receive their public financial aid when they get to college? Sadly, the answer is no. The Institute for College Access and Success (TICAS, 2010) estimated that California was leaving as much as $500 million on the table because community college students are not applying for Pell Grants. As more high schools adopt practices to help all graduating seniors complete their FAFSA, more students enrolling in community colleges will receive Pell Grants. The responsibility for helping students secure financial aid, however, does not end with high schools. TICAS suggests that attitudes, priorities, and management styles of financial aid offices can make a difference for students who must continue to apply while in college. Some colleges give student a "green light," encouraging their financial aid applications and others "create obstacles and 'red tape.'" It also found that limited resources are not predictive of what colleges help student secure financial aid. In other words, it is not a question of resources but of institutional priorities (TICAS, 2007).

Our experience confirms this. Using foundation data we looked at uptake in five community colleges that enrolled 30% of our students in the fall of 2012. Pell uptake rates for our students ranged from a perfect 100% to a low of 37%. BOG waivers granted ranged from 100% to 76%. Colleges with high Pell Grant uptake had high rates of BOG waivers granted; those with low Pell Grant rates also had BOG waiver rates. Finally, we looked at the student body composition. The two colleges where our students fared the worst were more than 60% Latino compared to the top performing colleges where Latinos were 17% or less of the student population.

When we highlight the challenges that our students face in securing financial aid, we have seen how community colleges improve their financial aid practices. Streamlining financial aid practices is a major first step. Using the experience of foundation scholars, one financial aid office was able to identify bottlenecks and streamline their practices. Providing financial aid information at every opportunity is another helpful practice. For example, incorporating information into freshmen orientation sessions can provide major benefits. By completing a FAFSA and applying for Cal Grants by March of their college freshman year, students have a second chance at a state entitlement grant. If they miss this opportunity, students should also be told, time and time again, that if they transfer to a four-year institution, they are eligible for Cal Grant transfer entitlement. As Maria reminds us, money management is a major challenge. Incorporating lessons on money management into orientation or other classes can be very helpful to students. At least one college tried issuing grant money in several installments, like a paycheck. Their experience may lead to a larger demonstration of its effectiveness.

Concluding Thoughts

The foundation believes that every eligible student should not just complete a financial aid application but also receive the financial aid they are entitled to. Our students are among the poorest in the state, which is why it is difficult to accept that not all are receiving public financial aid designed to help them pay for college. The differences among racial and ethnic groups also need to be probed and steps taken to close the gap. We want to place a spotlight on institutional practices in high schools and colleges. While community colleges have improved their Pell Grant uptake, from our experience, there is still too much variation among them (Santiago, 2012). Over the coming years, the foundation will continue to support efforts that make information about FAFSA completion rates, Cal Grant uptake, and other financial aid publicly available. Putting that information in the hands of students, parents, and local education and community college boards will help them monitor progress in their institutions. In the end, all of them are the people who can make change happen.

References

College Access Foundation of California. (2012, Spring). *Student Data Grantee Reference Deck.* Unpublished raw data (May 20, 2013).

Education Trust-West. (2013). *The cost of opportunity: Access to college financial aid in California.* Retrieved from http://www.edtrust.org/west/publication/the-cost-of -opportunity-access-to-college-financial-aid-in-california

Institute for Higher Education Leadership and Policy (IHELP). (2013). *Analysis of progress among CAFC Scholarship Recipients.* Unpublished report submitted to College Access Foundation of California.

Santiago, D. A. (2012, October). *How Latinos pay for college: Patterns of financial aid.* Presentation for NALEO Educational Summit, Washington, DC.

The Institute for College Access and Success (TICAS). (2007). *Green lights and red tape: Improving access to financial aid at California's community colleges.* Oakland, CA: Author.

The Institute for College Access and Success (TICAS). (2010). *Financial aid facts at California Community Colleges.* Oakland, CA: Author.

JULIA I. LOPEZ *is the president and CEO of the College Access Foundation of California.*

NEW DIRECTIONS FOR COMMUNITY COLLEGES • DOI: 10.1002/cc

INDEX

Accelerated developmental education, 39–41; acceleration models, 39–40; Community College of Baltimore County (CCBC), 41

Accelerated Study in Associate Programs (ASAP), 31

Achieving the Dream (ATD), 7; interventions across institutions, 14–15; Leadership Coaches and Data Coaches, 8–9; policies and practices of, 10–11; launch of, 8; role of boards in, 9–10; student progression, 10; transformative culture of, 11–13

Adams, P., 41

Allensworth, E., 33

American Historical Association (AHA), 63

Analytics, 19–21

Arizona State University (ASU), 29–30

Asera, R., 42

Ashby, J., 41

Asian students, 71

Bailey, T., 38, 39

Barefoot, B., 13

Basic Skills Initiative (BSI), 42

Belfield, C. R., 39

Berkner, L., 57

Bettinger, E. P., 38

Bill and Melinda Gates Foundation, 9, 72

Board of Trustees Institute (BOTI), 9

Boards, effective, 9–10

Bracco, K. R., 27, 28, 38, 40

Bradburn, E. M., 57

Bryk, A. S., 33

Bumphus, W. G., 2, 5, 6

Calcagno, J. C., 38

California Community College, 42

California Partnership for Achieving Student Success (Cal-PASS), 50

Career services and advising, 27

Carey, K., 29

Chapman, A., 3, 57, 65

Cho, S-W., 2, 27, 35, 38, 39, 41

Coaching for transformation, 8–9

Collado, H., 27

College Access Foundation of California, 67–68, 71–74

College Completion Agenda, 1, 39, 57; and data use, 17; and high schools, 47; strategies and solutions to advance, 1–2; and Tuning, 63–65

Common Core State Standards (CCSS), 47; colleges and, 49–50; development of, 48; primary goal of, 49–50

Community College Leadership Program (CCLP), 8–9

Community College of Baltimore County (CCBC) Accelerated Learning Program (ALP), 41

Community colleges: academic programs, 27–28; and four-year universities, 57–58; "guided pathways" approach to, 28; policy priority for, 37; reasons for choosing, 68–70; role of, 57; Tuning process, 59–60

Computer-adaptive instrument, 38

Covey, S., 21

Crosta, P., 28, 39

Curriculum alignment, 52–55; and college completion, 54–55; regional, 53–54; stages of, 52–53

Cutright, M., 13

Dadgar, 40

Data Coach, 8, 10

Data source, 18

Data use, 17–24; analytics, 19; analysis of data, 20; data collection, 19–20; human judgment and behavior, 21; decision making, 22; presentation of data, 22; organizational habits, 22; questions to be asked, 17; reporting, 20–21. *See also* IEBC Model.

Deil-Amen, R., 28

Developmental education reform, 42–44; Basic Skills Initiative (BSI), 42; in Connecticut, 43; in Florida, 43; in Virginia and North Carolina, 42–44

Edgecombe, N., 40

Educational pathways, 27

75

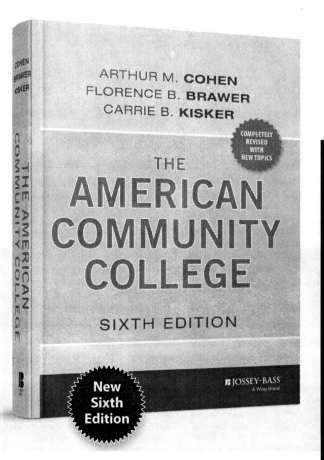

ARTHUR M. **COHEN**
FLORENCE B. **BRAWER**
CARRIE B. **KISKER**

COMPLETELY REVISED WITH NEW TOPICS

THE
AMERICAN COMMUNITY COLLEGE

SIXTH EDITION

New Sixth Edition

JB JOSSEY-BASS
A Wiley Brand

For over thirty years, *The American Community College* has provided up-to-date information and statistics about community colleges. It has been widely used in graduate courses and by community college scholars, institutional researchers, and on-the-ground administrators.

The sixth edition has been significantly updated with discussions of current issues including:

• Outcomes and accountability

• The rise of for-profit colleges

• Leadership and administrative challenges

• Revenue generation

• Distance learning

The book concludes with a cogent response to contemporary criticisms of the institution.

JB JOSSEY-BASS™
A Wiley Brand

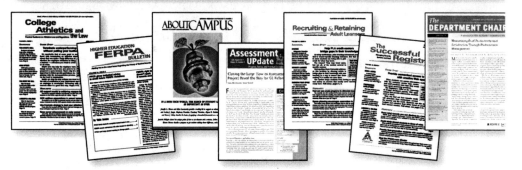

NEW DIRECTIONS FOR COMMUNITY COLLEGE
ORDER FORM SUBSCRIPTION AND SINGLE ISSUES

DISCOUNTED BACK ISSUES:

Use this form to receive 20% off all back issues of *New Directions for Community College*.
All single issues priced at **$23.20** (normally $29.00)

TITLE	ISSUE NO.	ISBN

Call 888-378-2537 or see mailing instructions below. When calling, mention the promotional code JBNND
to receive your discount. For a complete list of issues, please visit www.josseybass.com/go/ndcc

SUBSCRIPTIONS: (1 YEAR, 4 ISSUES)

☐ New Order   ☐ Renewal

U.S.	☐ Individual: $89	☐ Institutional: $311
CANADA/MEXICO	☐ Individual: $89	☐ Institutional: $351
ALL OTHERS	☐ Individual: $113	☐ Institutional: $385

Call 888-378-2537 or see mailing and pricing instructions below.
Online subscriptions are available at www.onlinelibrary.wiley.com

ORDER TOTALS:

Issue / Subscription Amount: $ _____

Shipping Amount: $ _____
(for single issues only – subscription prices include shipping)

Total Amount: $ _____

SHIPPING CHARGES:

First Item	$6.00
Each Add'l Item	$2.00

(No sales tax for U.S. subscriptions. Canadian residents, add GST for subscription orders. Individual rate subscriptions must
be paid by personal check or credit card. Individual rate subscriptions may not be resold as library copies.)

BILLING & SHIPPING INFORMATION:

☐ **PAYMENT ENCLOSED:** *(U.S. check or money order only. All payments must be in U.S. dollars.)*

☐ **CREDIT CARD:** ☐ VISA ☐ MC ☐ AMEX

Card number _____ Exp. Date _____

Card Holder Name _____ Card Issue # _____

Signature _____ Day Phone _____

☐ **BILL ME:** *(U.S. institutional orders only. Purchase order required.)*

Purchase order # _____
Federal Tax ID 13559302 • GST 89102-8052

Name _____

Address _____

Phone _____ E-mail _____

Copy or detach page and send to: **John Wiley & Sons, One Montgomery Street, Suite 1200, San Francisco, CA 94104-4594**

Order Form can also be faxed to: **888-481-2665**

PROMO JBNND

OTHER TITLES AVAILABLE IN THE
New Directions for Community Colleges
ARTHUR M. COHEN, EDITOR-IN-CHIEF
CAROLINE Q. DURDELLA AND NATHAN R. DURDELLA, ASSOCIATE EDITORS

CC163   Fostering the Liberal Arts in the 21st-Century Community College
Keith Kroll
The founding mission of the public, comprehensive community college
included vocational training, developmental education, community
education, and its collegiate function: transfer and the liberal arts. Early on in
its history, however, the community college's mission began to drift toward
vocational training to such an extent that at the local, state, and national
level the dominant narrative of the 21st-century community college portrays
a job (re)training center more than an educational institution. While
numerous books have described the growing threat to the liberal arts in
4-year colleges and universities, the response to "mission shift" within the
community college has been muted. This volume offers a timely,
much-needed, and persuasive argument for the importance of a liberal arts
education, particularly in the humanities, for all students attending a public,
comprehensive community college.
ISBN: 978-11188-34558

**CC162   The Future of the Urban Community College: Shaping the Pathways to a
Multiracial Democracy**
Gunder Myran, Curtis L. Ivery, Michael H. Parsons, Charles Kinsley
America's biggest cities are pulse points for the entire country. Already
weakened by decades of decline, their uneven recovery from the recent Great
Recession has resulted in the further concentration of prosperity in a few and
hardship for all the rest. Their citizens similarly reflect widening disparity
between the wealthiest and poorest, threatening an endangered middle class
that used to be the proudest measure of our economic and democratic ideals.
    Urban community colleges are undergoing rapid, multidimensional
changes in response to the new conditions and demands everywhere. The
challenge for all, regardless of size or location, is to reinvent themselves so
they can better meet the particular needs of their respective communities.
This national higher-education mandate is vital to democracy itself,
especially given the multiracial nature of metropolitan areas, where
challenges and opportunities have always been most pronounced.
    The future is as unpredictable as the events that brought us to this critical
juncture. Spurred by outside pressure and support as well as deep
commitment from within, urban colleges are vigorously exploring new
strategies for sustainability and success. In this volume, some of the most
prominent practitioners examine every major aspect of the
change-engagement process, including the role of governing boards,
workforce development, community partnerships, and redesign of outdated
business and finance models.
ISBN: 978-11188-06982

Statement of Ownership

Statement of Ownership, Management, and Circulation (required by 39 U.S.C. 3685), filed on OCTOBER 1, 2013 for NEW DIRECTIONS FOR COMMUNITY COLLEGES (Publication No. 0194-3081), published Quarterly for an annual subscription price of $89 at Wiley Subscription Services, Inc., at Jossey-Bass, One Montgomery St., Suite 1200, San Francisco, CA 94104-4594.

The names and complete mailing addresses of the Publisher, Editor, and Managing Editor are: Publisher, Wiley Subscription Services, Inc., A Wiley Company at San Francisco, One Montgomery St., Suite 1200, San Francisco, CA 94104-4594; Editor, Associate Editors- Caroline & Nathan Durdella Ph.D., Michael D. Eiser College of Education, CA State University, Northridge, 18111 Nordhoff Street, Northridge, CA 91330; Managing Editor, . . Contact Person: Joe Schuman; Telephone: 415-782-3232.

NEW DIRECTIONS FOR COMMUNITY COLLEGES is a publication owned by .Wiley Subscription Services, Inc., 111 River St., Hoboken, NJ 07030. The known bondholders, mortgages, and other security holders owning or holding 1% or more of total amount of bonds, mortgages, or other securities are(see list).

	Average No. Copies Each Issue During Preceding 12 Months	No. Copies Of Single Issue Published Nearest To Filing Date (Summer 2013)
15a. Total number of copies (net press run)	965	850
15b. Legitimate paid and/or requested distribution (by mail and outside mail)		
15b(1). Individual paid/requested mail subscriptions stated on PS form 3541 (include direct written request from recipient, telemarketing, and Internet requests from recipient, paid subscriptions including nominal rate subscriptions, advertiser's proof copies, and exchange copies)	398	382
15b(2). Copies requested by employers for distribution to employees by name or position, stated on PS form 3541	0	0
15b(3). Sales through dealers and carriers, street vendors, counter sales, and other paid or requested distribution outside USPS	0	0
15b(4). Requested copies distributed by other mail classes through USPS	0	0
15c. Total paid and/or requested circulation (sum of 15b(1), (2), (3), and (4))	398	382
15d. Nonrequested distribution (by mail and outside mail)		
15d(1). Outside county nonrequested copies stated on PS form 3541	127	126
15d(2). In-county nonrequested copies stated on PS form 3541	0	0
15d(3). Nonrequested copies distributed through the USPS by other classes of mail	0	0
15d(4). Nonrequested copies distributed outside the mail	0	0
15e. Total nonrequested distribution (sum of 15d(1), (2), (3), and (4))	127	126
15f. Total distribution (sum of 15c and 15e)	525	510
15g. Copies not distributed	440	340
15h. Total (sum of 15f and 15g)	965	850
15i. Percent paid and/or requested circulation (15c divided by 15f times 100)	76%	74.9%

I certify that all information furnished on this form is true and complete. I understand that anyone who furnishes false or misleading information on this form or who omits material or information requested on this form may be subject to criminal sanctions (including fines and imprisonment) and/or civil sanctions (including civil penalties).

Statement of Ownership will be printed in the Winter 2013 issue of this publication.

(signed) Susan E. Lewis, VP & Publisher-Periodicals

CPSIA information can be obtained at www.ICGtesting.com
Printed in the USA
BVOW05s2048010514

352281BV00005B/10/P